Contents

Introduction 1

Chapter 1
Vatican II: Human Autonomy and Christian Ethics 7

Chapter 2
Protestant Positions. The Questions of Natural Law
and the Law of Christ 29

Chapter 3
Christian Ethics and the Ecclesial Community 53

Chapter 4
Specific Christian Ethics and the Role of Tradition 68

Chapter 5
Christian Identity and Christian Ethics 93

Bibliography 123

Index 129

To My Students

IS THERE A CHRISTIAN ETHICS?

Lucien Richard, O.M.I.

Paulist Press
....
New York / Mahwah

The publisher is grateful to The University of Chicago Press and Basil Blackwell Ltd. for permission to reprint material from James Gustafson, *Ethics from a Theocentric Perspective, Volume I;* to The University of Chicago Press for permission to reprint material from James Gustafson, *Ethics from a Theocentric Perspective, Volume II* and *Protestant and Roman Catholic Ethics;* to Paulist Press for permission to reprint material from *The Distinctiveness of Christian Ethics*, Charles Curran and Richard McCormick, eds.; to Wm. B. Eerdmans Publishing Co. for permission to reprint material from *Documents of Vatican II*, Austin P. Flannery, ed., copyright © 1975 by Costello Co., Inc. and Rev. Austin Flannery, O.P.; to T & T Clark Ltd. for permission to reprint material from *Karl Barth, Church Dogmatics*, various volumes, G. W. Bromiley and T. F. Torrance, eds.

All rights reserved. No part of this book may be reproduced or transmitted in any form or by any means, electronic or mechanical, including photocopying, recording or by any information storage and retrieval system without permission in writing from the Publisher.

Library of Congress Cataloging-in-Publication Data

Richard, Lucien.
    Is there a Christian ethics?

    Bibliography: p.
    Includes index.
    1. Christian ethics—Catholic authors.   I. Title.
BJ1249.R478   1988   241   87-35685
ISBN 0-8091-2951-5 (pbk.)

Published by Paulist Press
997 Macarthur Boulevard
Mahwah, NJ 07430

Printed and bound in the
United States of America

Introduction

The area of contemporary Christian ethics is marked by a lively debate—is there a specifically Christian morality or ethic?[1] The debate is significant not only in the area of ethics but also in the larger theological context, for it touches the fundamental questions of Christology, anthropology, and soteriology. On the practical level, the debate raises the question of the relationship of Christianity and extra-Christian religious traditions. This question is of vital interest in the context of "world unification" or "planetization." Karl Jaspers has characterized this phenomenon in the following way: "What is historically new and for the first time in history decisive about our situation is the real unity of all. The planet has become a single whole dominated by the technology of communications; it is "smaller" than the Roman Empire was formerly."[2] The phenomenon of globalization entails serious challenges for the various religious traditions as they face the serious questions of nuclear war and social justice.

The question of the specificity of Christian ethics emerges at a time when fragmentation and pluralism characterize our culture.[3] The plu-

---

[1] cf. Charles E. Curran and Richard A. McCormick, eds. *The Distinctiveness of Christian Ethics. Readings in Moral Theology No. 2* (N.Y.: Paulist Press 1980).

[2] Karl Jaspers, *The Origin and Goal of History*. (New Haven: Yale University, 1953) p. 126. Cf. also Wilfred Cantwell Smith, *Towards a World Theology* (Philadelphia: Westminster, 1981).

[3] Langdon Gilkey, *Naming the Whirlwind: The Renewal of God-Language*. (Indianapolis: Bobbs-Merrill, 1969). Robert N. Bellah, ed. *Habits of the Heart* (Berkeley: University of California Press, 1985).

ralistic context is a new one; it involves a new consciousness and a new constructing of reality.[4] In a pluralistic consciousness there is no single way of interpreting or of knowing reality; there are many questions concerning life and its values and no single answer. The question of the specificity of Christian ethics emerges in a period when, more than at any previous time, Christianity is being challenged to provide some basis for moral action in society. Ethics is not simply for the private realm but also for the public; it includes public discourse.[5] However, in the context of the present culture not only must ethics recognize a plurality of "publics," but this plurality is often internalized in its own discourse. "Moral discussions," according to Robin W. Lovin, "are public in that they establish obligations that apply to persons generally, and they proceed by making generalizations about action."[6] Such a process underlines the question of whether there is a specific Christian ethics. Public moral discussions demand general participation whereas specific religious traditions concern particular individuals with particular beliefs. General and public participation in moral discourse implies the necessary quest for universal and general principles. Within a religious community, there is always a tendency to claim that such principles are sanctioned by God.

The importance of the question of whether there is a specific Christian ethics has become more evident in the United States. Generalizations about values and goals have become the norm in the secular culture; whereas, in a religious tradition, more specific ideas and beliefs about values and goals prevail. To speak about a Christian ethics is to underline the point that ethics is an activity that relates to particular times, individuals, places, and communities. To speak about the publicness of ethics is to underline the universal claim of particular ethics. The 1980

---

[4]John Cobb, *The Structure of Christian Existence* (Philadelphia: Westminster, 1967). Karl Rahner "Pluralism in Theology and the Oneness of the Church's Profession of Faith," *The Development of Fundamental Theology*, ed. Johann Baptist Metz, Concilium 46 (New York: Paulist Press, 1969). David Tracy, *Blessed Rage for Order* (New York: Seabury, 1975) 3–21 and *The Analogical Imagination* (New York: Crossroad, 1981) 366ff.

[5]cf. David Tracy, *The Analogical Imagination, op. cit.*, p. 4. On the publicness of theology pp. 4–46. Joseph Monti, *Ethics and Public Policy: The Conditions of Public Moral Discourse* (Washington: University of America Press, 1982).

[6]Robin W. Lovin, *Christian Faith and Public Choices. The Social Ethics of Barth, Bronner and Bonhoeffer* (Philadelphia: Fortress Press, 1984) p. 5.

electoral campaign which brought Ronald Reagan and his conservative followers to power produced some original and far-reaching changes in American religious and political life. It witnessed the entrance of the "New Christian Right" into the political arena. Religious denominations have long been active participants in the political struggle to develop and direct public policy,[7] but we are now witnessing a new and more local participation of religious groups. The "New Christian Right" has created what is known as "The Politics of Moralism." While morality is an ongoing search for the needed criteria to establish the rightness or wrongness of human action, "Moralism" posits only one correct moral answer to any ethical problem and bases its criteria on the absolute authority of Scripture.[8] The emergence of this movement raises important questions for a religiously pluralistic society. The questions go beyond this particular movement, for they are directly related to the role of religion, and more specifically of Christianity, in morality: what function does Christianity have in determining criteria for moral action? Is Christianity fundamentally divisive in the realm of morality?

Christianity represents a spectrum of positions varying from the "New Christian Right" to the radical, Marxist-inspired Christian left. Yet these positions share the basic assumption that God cannot be restricted to the private sector. Issues of social justice, human rights and peace have to be understood and resolved in terms of a theologically based ethics and anthropology. This consensus, however, cannot conceal deep-seated disagreements among various Christian groups, as shown in their total lack of consensus when proposing practical solutions to specific problems. More theoretically, the problematic nature of this apparent consensus is revealed at the meta-ethical level where fundamental questions are raised.

The meta-ethical level relative to Christian ethics is Christology. Here again, the context is pluralistic.[9] Yet, what characterizes many of the various positions in the debate is Christocentrism.[10] Such a Chris-

---

[7]P. J. Weber, "Examining the Religious Lobbies," *This World* No. 1 (1982) pp. 97–107.

[8]Erling Jorstad, *The Politics of Moralism*, (Minneapolis, Augsburg, 1981).

[9]Charles A. Wilson, "Christology and the Pluralist Consciousness," *Word and World*, (Winter, 1985 No. 1) pp. 68–77.

[10]On Christocentrism, cf. Eugene TeSelle, *Christ in Context: Divine Purpose and*

tocentric position is well expressed by Dietrich Bonhoeffer writing about human dignity: "It is nothing else than bondage to Jesus Christ alone, completely breaking through every program and every set of laws. No other significance is possible since Jesus is the only significance. Beside Jesus nothing has any significance. He alone matters."[11] There are a variety of ways of understanding "Christocentrism" or "Christomonism"[12] but at the most fundamental level one could define these terms as presupposing that the Incarnation is the center and aim of creation and of all God's activity toward the world.

A Christocentric approach emphasizes the uniqueness, originality, and unsurpassable nature of the revelation of God in the person of Jesus Christ. Not only is God fully revealed only through Jesus Christ but there is also a shared affirmation that what humanness is can be discovered only in the person of Jesus. Certain affirmations of the Constitution *Gaudium et Spes* seem to underline this belief. The Constitution constantly and pressingly presents Jesus Christ as the "new humanity" and the true answer to the mystery of human destiny.[13] Jesus Christ is presented as

---

Human Possibility (Philadelphia: Fortress Press, 1975); Jean Milet, *God or Christ—The Excesses of Christocentricity* (New York: Crossroad, 1981).

[11] Dietrich Bonhoeffer, *The Cost of Discipleship* (New York: Macmillan, 1963), p. 49.

[12] According to Eugene TeSelle, Christocentrism can be understood "sometimes merely in an epistemological framework, viewing Jesus of Nazareth as the 'paradigmatic event' in relation to which all events in human history are interpreted (the Niebuhrs); sometimes in an anthropological framework, viewing him as the center of the history of the human race (Schleiermacher); sometimes in an entire ontological framework, viewing him as the raison d'etre of the entire cosmos . . . ", E. TeSelle, *Christ in Context, op. cit.,* p. 1.

[13] Christianity proclaims that in Christ the human ideal for which all men strive has been attained in history and, in fact, that unless one is a man as Christ was a man, one cannot be a man at all. Jesus is not only the revelation of God but also the revelation of man. In him the question as to who is God and who is man are answerable only in their complementarity, not as two questions but as one. The Constitution *Gaudium et Spes* affirms this truth in many ways: "In reality it is only in the mystery of the Word made flesh that the mystery of man truly becomes clear. For Adam, the first man, was a type of him Who was to come, namely Christ the Lord, the new Adam, in the very revelation of the mystery of the Father and of his love, fully reveals man to himself and brings to light his most high calling." From *Gaudium et Spes,* in *Vatican Council II: The Conciliar and Post Conciliar Documents,* ed. Austin Flannery (Collegeville, Minn.: Liturgical Press, 1975), p. 922.

the one who decodes the mystery which human reality is to itself. Such claims about the person of Jesus Christ have led to claims about the supremacy of Christianity in relation to other religious traditions and of Christian ethics over any other form of ethics. One representative claim can be found in the writings of Heinrich Kraemer: "The Christian ethic . . . is entirely incommensurate with all other ethics in the world. All ethics in the world except the Christian ethics are some form of preparation."[14] And the author affirms that only in Christianity is the love of the neighbor, without condition, taught.

This Christocentric approach is now under attack from an ethical perspective. In his book *Christ in a Changing World: Toward an Ethical Christology,* Tom Driver attempts a "convergence between ethical conscience and Christic expectation in our day and time."[15] It is Driver's contention that most of our Christologies promote unethical forms of behavior such as sexism and anti-Semitism.[16] Dorothee Soelle characterizes much of contemporary Christology as "Christofascism."[17] While the question of the specificity of Christian ethics is a difficult one in itself, the complexity of the question is compounded by the various contexts in which it is posed. We shall enter the debate from within the Roman Catholic tradition.

---

[14] Heinrich Kraemer. *The Christian Message in a Non-Christian World,* (Grand Rapids: Kregal, 1963), p. 86.

[15] Tom F. Driver, *Christ In a Changing World: Toward an Ethical Christology* (New York: Crossroad, 1981).

[16] cf. Rosemary R. Ruether, *Faith and Fratricide,* (New York: Seabury, 1974).

[17] Dorothy Soelle, *Suffering* (Philadelphia: Fortress, 1975) pp. 22ff.

Vatican II: Human Autonomy and Christian Ethics

Within the Roman Catholic context, it was in light of the Constitution *Gaudium et Spes* that the question of a specifically Christian ethic emerged. Vatican II was fundamentally an attempt at renewal of the Roman Catholic church and at dialogue with a contemporary and secularized world.[18] The theologians at Vatican II made frequent reference to the pluralism of society and to the Church's need to be relevant to society. They said the Church was being forced to move towards an open Catholicism, in dialogue not only with all other Christians but with extra-Christians and even anti-Christians.[19] Many moral theologians saw this opening on the part of the Church as an invitation to highlight the communicable dimensions of the Christian tradition. In order to realize this perceived mandate, they brought together two elements, one contemporary and the other more traditional. They saw the importance of secularization as affirmation of the autonomy of creation. In *Gaudium et Spes* they perceived a qualified understanding of autonomy. Created things have their own laws and have to be understood in themselves. Yet it is through creation that such autonomy emerges and therefore though created reality has its autonomy and value such is never independent of

---

[18]cf. Langdon Gilkey, *Catholicism Confronts Modernity. A Protestant View.* (New York: Crossroad, 1975).

[19]cf. Karl Rahner, "Christianity and the Non-Christian Religions," *Theological Investigations* 5 (London: Darton, Longman and Todd, 1966), pp. 115–134.

God.[20] These moral theologians also built on the classical Thomistic tradition concerning autonomous reason.

The debate on the specificity of Christian ethics was opened by Auer in Germany.[21] The debate led to a series of polemical discussions between two opposing camps: those who upheld an autonomous morality within a Christian context and those who upheld a faith ethic. The first group considered moral theology to be strictly rational and autonomous in relation to faith and religion. The opposing party viewed reason as too weak to arrive at any certainty in the area of moral norms.[22] In the United States the debate was joined by Charles Curran, who published in 1974 an essay entitled "Is There a Catholic and/or Christian Ethic?"[23]

In the history of Christian ethics, few have denied that there is some relationship between faith and morality. What is being debated is the precise nature of that dependence.[24] The question of the specificity of Christian ethics also leads us into a different, but not totally unrelated, area. The question of a specific Christian ethics demands the isolation of the distinctive or specifically Christian elements. This task cannot be achieved without reference to the existence and nature of a specifically Christian canon and sources of moral wisdom for the Christian believer. The Christian is in possession of various theological beliefs, a complex of symbols and various liturgical practices which lead to a specific way of understanding the world. What role does this understanding have in a situation where an ethical response to a specific question is required? It is usually understood by Christians that there are appropriate and inappropriate Christian responses in such situations, and that faith is a source that can be called upon to help a believer decide. The questions then emerge: How is faith integrated with the moral reasoning process? What is its relationship to reason? How autonomous are the two? It is with these questions that the debate began.

---

[20]*Gaudium et Spes*, No. 36, p. 935.

[21]A. Auer, *Autonome Moral und Christlicher Glaube*, (Dusseldorf: Patmos-Verlag, 1971).

[22]cf. Jean Marie Aubert, "Débats autour de la Morale Fondamentale," *Studia Moralia* 20 (1982), pp. 95–122.

[23]Charles Curran, "Is There a Catholic and/or Christian Ethic?" *Proceedings of the Catholic Theological Society of America* 29 (1974) pp. 125–154.

[24]cf. James W. Walter, "Christian Ethics: Distinctive and Specific," *American Ecclesiastical Review* 169 (1975), pp. 470–489.

According to Auer, autonomous persons exist as such in virtue of their grounding in a transcendent origin (protology) and also in their ultimate end defined as a communion with the God of Jesus who is attainable only in the world to come (eschatology). Auer's position is linked to a specific understanding of God's causal agency. God's divine transcendence is operative throughout human history and particularly in the Incarnation. Further, it directs everything toward the eschaton although it does so in such a way that human existence, though deeply permeated, is not transformed into something else. In fact God's transcendent presence exalts human freedom and its potential to such an extent that whatever development occurs, historical or ethical, belongs simultaneously to God and to humankind. Human autonomy is God's gift so that humanity may respond freely to God's call to love and perfection.[25]

Within that perspective the author argues for a morality that is to be rationally autonomous relative to concrete norms, but enriched through faith with a greater understanding. Through this enlarged understanding, the believer can perceive deeper meanings to subjective experience and discern values often disregarded by others. The faith-enlarged understanding works in an autonomous morality by means of a process of motivation. Faith demands an integration of an autonomous morality and this understanding, which can lead to concrete actions.[26]

Autonomous Morality and the Centrality of Jesus Christ

This thesis of an autonomous morality is basically accepted by most European Roman Catholic theologians, including Bruno Schuller, Joseph Fuchs, Edward Schillebeeckx, and Hans Küng. While these theologians affirm the same thesis, each does so in his own particular way.

It is significant that Joseph Fuchs, the most influential of these authors, entered the debate on the specificity of Christian ethics with a book on natural law. In *Natural Law: A Theological Investigation*,[27] he at-

---

[25] Enda McDonagh, *Gift and Call*, (St. Meinrad, Indiana: Abbey Press, 1975).

[26] On this position cf: D. Mieth and F. Compagnoni, *Ethik im Kontext des Glaubens*, (Fribourg, 1978).

[27] Joseph Fuchs. *Natural Law: A Theological Investigation*, (New York: Sheed and Ward, 1965).

tempted to clarify the theological foundations of natural law. His approach is formally Christological. In developing his argument, Fuchs reiterates the classical position that humanity is created in the image of God. Within his Christological perspective of natural law, creation plays an important role, for creation was from the beginning oriented to the Incarnation. According to the author, "Scripture in fact tells us that in him and for him all things were created . . . "[28] Jesus Christ "is our prototype because he is truly man and realizes in himself the essence of man's natural being, no more and no less than we do."[29] While the fall weakened the human intellect and will, the image of God in which we are created and on which natural law is founded is not destroyed. Since creation is intrinsically connected with Incarnation, there must be some continuity between human nature and Christ's grace; what happens in the redemption cannot bring about a reality that is totally different from that which is present and given in creation. Whatever is necessary to an ethical existence is already given with the gift of our humanness. Whatever is revealed in the person of Jesus about being human adds nothing new to what can be discovered through our own reason. What Christ does is to empower us to arrive at an authentic humanity. Human nature, while autonomous, needs to be touched by divine reality; that touching occurs at the depth of human existence and transforms the moral agent.

Joseph Fuchs makes a distinction between the material and the formal element in Christian ethics, a distinction between the transcendent and categorical dimensions. In Fuchs, each moral, ethical decision is a specific and determinate one realized and accomplished in a reflexive way. Yet each action promotes the becoming of the person, the emerging of personhood which occurs often in a non-thematic or non-reflexive way. This emergence of personhood can only be arrived at ultimately in a personal relationship with the Absolute Person who is God. For a Christian this relationship can be understood as a relationship to Jesus Christ. This implies a certain intentionality that one can describe as Christian, whereas the specific moral acts are fundamentally and categorically the same for everyone. The material content of Christian intentionality remains the demand of human morality as such. According

---

[28]Ibid., p. 74.
[29]Ibid., p. 75.

to the author, "Christian intentionality . . . is to be seen as the most important and decisive element of Christian morality." In its categorical dimension, in its determinate aspect, "Christian morality is basically and substantially a *humanum*, a morality of genuine being-human."[30] There cannot be at this level any opposition of the Sermon on the Mount to the *humanum*. In a sense, then, one must speak of a basic human element as well as a specifically Christian element in Christian morality.[31] To the human element as such belongs the radical openness to a relationship with God, and therefore God's accessibility. To the specifically Christian element belongs a more explicit expression of that openness. The difference between the two in Fuchs' thought is primarily the Christian understanding of the Revelation which is already present.[32] The human and Christian elements are not in contradiction to one another: one is essentially open to the other. This position is anchored in a transcendental and anthropological approach both to ethics and to Christology. As such it is more faithful to the natural law orientation, although it perceives the natural law in a more dynamic way than formerly. What is underlined by this position is the basic continuity of creation and Incarnation. Since from the beginning there is essentially only one order, human existence, from the very beginning human beings are called to God and must take a position for or against God. Human existence in its ontological structure is historically and concretely addressed and called to a decision for God.

Fuchs' approach to ethics is Christological, but in a special sense. What we have here is a two-layered approach to morality. For example, a Christian will perform an act of justice for the same reasons as any other person, but the Christian will do so out of a Christian motivation. According to Fuchs, "Christian motivation provides human conduct

---

[30]Joseph Fuchs, "Is There a Specifically Christian Morality?" *The Distinctiveness of Christian Ethics, op. cit.* p. 8.

[31]Ibid. p. 2.

[32]Fuchs writes: The "Christian-ness" of radical openness vis a vis God's salvific call may therefore also be explained as follows. First: The clear and explicit awareness of man's true relationship, as man, to God cannot be achieved easily by him—the "man of the fall"—without Christian revelation; Christian anthropology provides an excellent help for man's deeper knowledge about himself. Secondly: only in faith in the God who reveals himself do we experience that God's personal call to us is indeed a call to salvation. *Ibid.*, p. 14.

with a deeper and richer meaning and is subjectively part of the action itself."[33] But at the categorical level, norms for justice are the same for everyone and can be known by everyone through natural law. While Fuchs' position is Christological, it gives natural law an important role and leads to the affirmation that, in reference to its transcendental dimension, the moral life can be viewed as distinctively Christian. However, on the categorical level, Christian ethics is not distinctively Christian. What is normatively Christian and what is normatively human are convertible. Fuchs places great emphasis on, and confidence in, the goodness of what is genuinely or normatively human. That which is fully human is ultimately Christian. Within this perspective, Scripture as a source of ethical knowledge does not offer basically new information, but functions more as a "reminder of" or as "exhortation to" the genuinely human.

In his approach, Fuchs poses the important question of the role of Scripture in ethics. It would seem that Christianity's claim to distinctiveness must somehow be grounded in the fact of the canonicity of its Scriptures. The question of the specificity of Christian ethics cannot avoid the question of the role of Scripture.[34] While Fuchs merely poses the question, Bruno Schuller, another European Roman Catholic theologian, deals directly with it in detail.[35] He follows Fuchs in affirming that on the categorical level there is no distinctive Christian ethics. It is at this level that Scripture must be seen in its relation to ethics. According to Schuller, biblical ethics is exhortatory but "does not convey any new moral insights."[36] What we are given in the New Testament is a model to follow. Yet, as the author points out, a model is a standard developed from the norms whereas the requirements of morality are the norms themselves.[37] In other words, these latter requirements pre-exist the model, "Only if we suppose that human persons already experience

---

[33]Ibid., p. 15.

[34]What is being dealt with here is the more formal aspect of the role of Scripture in relation to ethics. On the ethical content of the New Testament cf.: Bruce C. Birch and Larry L. Rasmussen, *Bible and Ethics in the Christian Life*, (Minneapolis, Augsburg Publications, 1976).

[35]Bruno Schuller, "The Debate on the Specific Character of a Christian Ethics: Some Remarks," in *The Distinctiveness of Christian Ethics, op. cit.*, pp. 207–233.

[36]Ibid., p. 216.

[37]Ibid., p. 213.

themselves as called to be morally good, can God appear to them as a model to be unconditionally imitated once they have recognized him as the absolute embodiment of moral goodness."[38] The Scriptures are related to the normativity of ethics not in a fundamental, causal way, but as exhortation and motivation. Exhortation "of itself does not convey any new moral insights, but it does have or is intended to have, the result that the person addressed allows its moral insights to touch him personally and that he hear them as a challenge to be converted, do penance, change his life and act as he knows he ought to act."[39] While scriptural exhortation and motivation may deepen one's grasp of ethical values such as justice and love, it is not constitutive of their moral validity. It is essential to distinguish carefully between the genesis and the truth value of an ethical norm. It by no means follows from this that the demands of morality as lived and interpreted by Jesus take us beyond the realm of knowledge accessible to reason. From the theological viewpoint the requirements of morality, insofar as they are accessible in principle to natural reason, are commandments of the Creator. If we keep this in mind it is not clear how anyone can show that Jesus did not intend simply to revalidate the commandments of the Creator against possible misunderstandings. As moral exhortation, Scripture does not face the theologian as a source whose authority is absolute and without context. The cultural conditioning of Scripture leads to a flexibility in the appreciation of many of its imperatives.

The Influence of Karl Rahner

The positions previously described have clearly been influenced by the theology of Karl Rahner. Compared to the amount Rahner wrote on the subject of systematic theology, his writings on ethics appear somewhat minimal.[40] His impact in the area of ethics and on the question of

---

[38]Ibid.

[39]Ibid., p. 216.

[40]On Rahner's ethics see: D. J. Dorr, "Karl Rahner's Formal Existentialist Ethics," *Irish Theological Quarterly* 36, (1969), pp. 221–229. James F. Bresnahan, "Rahner's Christian Ethics," *America* 123, (1970), pp. 351–354. Ronald Modras, "Implications of Rahner's Anthropology for Fundamental Moral Theology," *Horizons*, (1985), 70–90.

the specificity of Christian ethics comes from his contribution in systematic theology, primarily in Christology and anthropology.

The beginning point for understanding Rahner's contribution is his anthropology. This anthropology is decidedly influenced by Joseph Marechal and involves a "turn to the subject and a transcendental method."[41]

Rahner's reflection on the peculiarly transcendental character of human subjectivity uncovers a universally experienced directedness toward God, who is offering intimacy to all. The human experience of openness to the infinite and of the dynamic drive toward the absolute are normatively human. The divine transcendence is historically concretized and expressed in the Incarnation and is operative throughout human history. God's salvific will has always been offered to all humanity. There never has been a reality which could be called purely human. Christian revelation and faith-experience make explicit for the Christian what is already present implicitly in common human experience. Rahner can write:

> a direct presence of God belongs to the nature of a spiritual person in the sense of an unsystematic attunement and an unreflected horizon which determines everything else within which the whole spiritual life of this spirit is lived. This direct presence of God belongs to the nature of a spiritual person as the ground which, though not allowing us to grasp it completely in a reflexive manner, is nevertheless the permanent basis for all other spiritual activities and which on this ac-

---

[41] Marechal's position is summarized in the following way by Gerald McCool: "A real dynamism demands that its goal or term also be real. It follows therefore that, if the mind's real striving toward the Infinite Absolute is one of the a priori conditions of the speculative reason's objective judgments, God's real existence is an a priori condition of possibility for every categorical judgment of the speculative reason. From this discovery two others immediately follow. Firstly, far from showing that the idea of God is merely a regulative ideal for speculative reason, a transcendental reflection on human knowledge manifests that God's real existence is an a priori condition of possibility for any speculative judgment whatsoever. Thus a judgment which doubts or denies his existence is a contradiction and destroys itself in its very utterance. Secondly, since God's real existence as First Cause is a necessary condition of possibility for any speculative judgment whatsoever, the judgments of speculative reason are **metaphysical affirmations.**" Taken from Gerald A. McCool (ed.), *A Rahner Reader* (New York: Seabury, 1975), pp. xiv–xv.

count is always more 'there,' though less there as object, and less objectively 'there' than everything else.[42]

Through God's creative act, the human emerges as a being with whom God can achieve self-communication without ceasing to be God.

Again Rahner writes:

> God is not to be thought of as merely over against the world and its history in virtue of simply being its first cause, untouched by the world itself and transcending it. Rather in the outward movement of his love he has inserted himself into the world as its innermost *entelechia* and he impels the whole of this world and its history towards that point at which God himself will be the innermost and immediately present fulfillment of our existence in the face-to-face presence of eternal beatitude.[43]

While this view of creation means that God is immanent in creation, and that creation's nature is directed towards God, it also means that God does not have to intervene from outside creation. The expression "from outside" applied to God's creating and even to God's revelation is not an adequate one. God never really acts in anything from outside because God is present in everything that exists as the deepest foundation of that existence. God is not encompassed by creation but is certainly always more deeply present to it than that reality is to itself.

Through God's act of creation, reality is established as truly different from, although always derived from God. The divine self-gift is such that what is established is established precisely in its difference from God. Creation is the establishment, by God, of what is other, precisely as other. There is an authentic autonomy of all earthly realities, but never an independence from God. Because of the unity of nature and grace from the very beginning of creation, the history of the world and salvation history are materially identical and coextensive; yet salvation history, being the result of a free and internal response to God's self-

---

[42] K. Rahner, "Dogmatic Reflections on the Knowledge and Self-Consciousness of Christ," in *Theological Investigations*, 5, p. 209.

[43] K. Rahner, "Christology in the Setting of Modern Man's Understanding of Himself and of His World," in *Theological Investigations*, 5, p. 20.

communication, is never fully objectified. To this autonomous world history, God is self-giving. This self-gift, accepted and received, manifests itself in this one profane, secular, autonomous world. Although the orders of grace and nature are not identical, there is only one creative intention on the part of the Creator, namely redeeming self-communication. As Rahner writes: "In the concrete order of supernatural divine self-communication as in fact willed by God, every natural created entity is ordered to this grace in such a way that it cannot remain really whole and healthy in itself, nor achieve the completion required by its own nature, except as integrated into the supernatural order of grace. In the concrete order, then, nature itself can find its way to its own completion only if it realizes that it is actually a factor within the all-embracing reality of grace and redemption."[44] Again Rahner writes: "Instead of placing the orders of redemption and creation alongside each other, we speak of the order of redemption *within* the order of creation; this states the thesis that divine grace, the fruit of redemption, actually penetrates the created order itself, healing and sanctifying it; that it incorporates the world, in all its abiding naturality, into the *mysterium Christi;* and that this process of taking the world by grace into the life of God is also meant, according to God's will, to be carried out by the activity of men."[45]

For Rahner, the natural and the supernatural orders are radically one. The order of redemption is neither against nor above creation. "The two orders are then still, indeed, not identical, but neither are they adequately distinguishable from each other; they are related as the whole to the part."[46] The relation is one of unity without identity; yet Rahner does emphasize the priority of grace over nature.

Rahner's position is not without tension. Salvation is from God and therefore in some way relativizes human history and achievements; yet this salvation takes place in this world. World history and therefore human autonomy appear to be devalued, yet this world and profane history are absolutized. It is from within this tension that one can understand Rahner's concept of grace. There is always a vertical and a horizontal dimension to grace. As Roger Haight writes: "In the experience of

---

[44] Karl Rahner, "The Order of Redemption Within the Order of Creation," *The Christian Commitment* (New York: Sheed and Ward, 1963), p. 50.
[45] Ibid., pp. 38–39.
[46] Ibid., p. 41.

grace, Christians are in touch with eternity in their transcendent acts of freedom. And in that experience they experience as well the essential finitude of everything in this world and of every future in it."[47]

Rahner's anthropology has important implications in the field of ethics. With his transcendental anthropology, Rahner indicated that the grounds of morality have deeper roots than suspected. Since God is so deeply present in human existence, Rahner can say: "We meet God everywhere in a most radical way as the most basic question of our freedom, in all things of the world and (in the words of Scripture) above all in our neighbor."[48] Human freedom in this framework "is the capacity for the eternal."[49] Again Rahner writes: "The only ultimate structure of the person which manages to express it completely is the basic capacity of love, and this without measure. Thus man too is boundless. Every sin is at root merely the refusal to entrust himself to this boundlessness; it is a lesser love which, because it refuses to become the greater, is no longer love at all."[50]

In discussing human freedom, Rahner uses the language of anthropology. "In contradistinction to 'things,' which are always complete and which are moved from one mode of completion to another and thus are at the same time always in a final state and yet never ultimate, man begins his existence as the being who is radically open and incomplete. When his essence is complete it is as he himself has freely completed it."[51] Human essence is freedom, and according to Rahner, such freedom has broad possibilities.

> Man, as the being who is free in relation to God, is in a most radical way empowered to do what he wills with himself, freely able to align himself towards his own ultimate goal. He is able so to determine and dispose of himself that two absolutely different final destinations become possible: man in absolute salvation and man in the absolute loss

---

[47] Roger Haight, *The Experience and Language of Grace*, (New York: Paulist Press, 1979), p. 135.

[48] Karl Rahner, "Theology of Freedom," in *Theological Investigations* no. 6 (New York: Seabury, 1974), pp. 181–182.

[49] Ibid.

[50] Ibid., p. 188.

[51] Karl Rahner, "The Experiment with Man," in *Theological Investigation*, vol. 9, trans. Graham Harrison (New York: Herder and Herder, 1972), p. 213.

of salvation . . . This freedom is creative and what it creates is man himself in his final state, so that the beginning of this history of man's divinely appointed freedom—man's "essence" as we say—is not an intangible something, essentially permanent and complete, but the commission and power which enable him to be free to determine himself to his ultimate state.[52]

God is present in every act of freedom as its ground and goal.[53] Freedom in its nature is the transcendent power which makes possible self-actualization, the fundamental condition for self-giving love. Rahner distinguishes between transcendental freedom and freedom of choice. Trancendental freedom is that freedom which lies at the very core of human existence and which is exercised in various historical moments.

Because human beings are historical and social beings, their God-given openness and emergence must be actualized in the world and in history. There is no actual knowledge of God and no true response to God except as it is actualized in the world and in history. Humanity's transcendental essence comes to be and achieves actuality in time and space; it has no existence of its own apart from the physical universe and from human history. Hence, Rahner emphasizes that humanity is indeed transcendence and spirit, but only in and through the particularities of individual and social structures and histories. We are touched in and through historical situations, and while there are some transcendental values that are permanently valid, human nature does change. Human freedom involves the possibility and responsibility of change.

Rahner's understanding of the transcendental structure of human existence is bound to affect his understanding of natural law. Natural law is embedded in the supernatural existential. In this way humanity exists in both nature and "supernature." Since it is difficult to know precisely the limits of human nature, the same will be true of natural law. Natural law cannot be understood in rigid forms. The meaning of human life is not already given in some pre-existing pattern or place. Rather, it is to be found creatively in life and experience, where the moral subject plays an important role. Moral action is not simply the realization of a universal norm; it does not exclude particularity and individuality.

---

[52]Ibid., p. 212.
[53]Karl Rahner, "Theology of Freedom," *op. cit.*, p. 180.

> In so far as man belongs to the material world by his concrete activity, his activity is an instance and fulfillment of something different from the individual and opposed to it, i.e., as a *law* expressed in universal propositions. In so far as the same man subsists in his own spirituality, his actions are also always more than mere applications of the universal law to the *casus* in space and time; they have a substantial positive property and uniqueness which can no longer be translated into a universal idea and norm expressible in propositions constructed of universal notions.[54]

Natural law does not eliminate human freedom and creativity. In the same way that human nature is a radical question to be answered by God, natural law is also a question whose answer is to be found in God's self-communication in the Person of Jesus Christ.

Natural law, knowable and acted upon by all human beings, is, according to Rahner, graced and therefore Christian, for it is created in and for Christ. So in a real sense, all ethics are Christian ethics, all morality is Christian morality. Rahner's contribution to the question of the specificity of Christian ethics is a coherent Christology and anthropology. But as we shall later see, this contribution is not without question and tension.[55]

Schillebeeckx: Christology and Ethics

Edward Schillebeeckx is another European Roman Catholic theologian who has contributed to the debate on the question of the specificity of Christian ethics. While the main concern of his work is not precisely ethics, his contribution relates to the grounding of ethics and has been primarily in the area of Christology.[56]

For Schillebeeckx, ethics within the Christian context is the expression of grace as mediated historically in and through Jesus Christ. Schil-

---

[54] Karl Rahner, "On the Question of a Formal Existential Ethics," *Theological Investigations*, no. 2 (London: Darton, Longman and Todd, 1964), p. 226.

[55] For an evaluation of Rahner's contribution in ethics see: Richard McCormick, "Does Faith Add to Ethical Perception?," *The Distinctiveness of Christian Ethics, op. cit.*, p. 162.

[56] William P. George, "The Praxis of the Kingdom of God: Ethics in Schillebeeckx' *Jesus and the Christ*", *Horizons*, (1985), pp. 44–69.

lebeeckx does not see Jesus primarily as an ethics teacher nor as a political reformer, but rather as an eschatological prophet whose identity is of important ethical and political significance.

According to Schillebeeckx, "Jesus is the eschatological prophet of God's time of mercy."[57] The whole focus of his mission is that of service to the other.[58] That mission is expressed in his preaching and message, which is about the kingdom of God.[59] This message is expressed in parables that demand a response of conversion and action on the part of the audience. Jesus is himself a parable confronting us "with the question whether or not we also wish, venture, and are able to see in Jesus' activity a manifestation of God's regard for people."[60] To say that Jesus is the eschatological prophet is to say that while his life seems to have ended in failure, the cross, that same historical cross is the locus from which the promise of salvation is historically spoken and historically effected.

That salvation affects us now, through our discipleship. Christian identity, i.e., the promise of salvation in Jesus Christ as historically mediated, is correlative to Jesus' own identity. That identity is perceived by Schillebeeckx as that of the eschatological prophet whose mission is to serve others and to summon his audience to unconditional love for all. This mission entails specific actions which are determined by historical situations.[61] The truth of any response to Christ's message must somehow be correlative to Jesus' own praxis. This praxis becomes a challenge for ethical behavior.

There is no complete vision of God's reign, no complete grasp of the nature or of the future of humanity. We have a fragmentary and limited grasp, for the eschatological prophet himself had a "distant vision of a final, perfect, and universal salvation . . . in and through his own fragmentary actions, which were historical and thus limited or finite."[62]

---

[57] Edward Schillebeeckx, *Jesus: An Experiment in Christology*, (New York: Crossroad, 1978), p. 499.
[58] Ibid., p. 303.
[59] Ibid., p. 154.
[60] Ibid., p. 170.
[61] Ibid., p. 669–741.
[62] Edward Schillebeeckx, *Christ: The Experience of Jesus as Lord*, (New York: Crossroad, 1980), p. 791.

It is in our fragmented life that discipleship continues Jesus' own identity. That identity is completely wrapped up in Jesus' own ministry of service to others and ultimately in suffering for and with the other, a suffering that can be called compassion.

Jesus' compassion is an expression and revelation of God's own compassion and therefore of God's solidarity with us. In Exodus, God's name is "solidarity with my people."[63] Grace is that solidarity, and as such grace is the offer of a future to those without a future. Such grace is the foundation and grounding of ethics, i.e., Christian ethics. Through such grace, men and women are freed for ethical life and commitment. The nature of such a commitment is made known in the New Testament, which "gives us the most direct, uniquely practicable and historical, most reliable event, the Christian movement that took its impetus from Jesus of Nazareth."[64]

Ethics is no longer, in the New Testament, an ethic of the categorical imperative, of commandments and prohibitions; it is not even a value ethic or an ethic of virtue. It is an ethic which rests on the "*iustitia Dei*, that is, on God's action in creating salvation," on God's prerogative to bring about righteousness on earth. Life as an eschatological gift is given to us as a new creation, and therefore we can also live in accord with the demands of the reign of God.

Ethical life, in its micro- and macro-ethical dimensions, is the recognizable content of salvation, the historical manifestation or demonstration of the imminence of the reign of God. Therefore, the reign of God and ethics are intrinsically connected. The religious manifests itself in the ethical, and as a result transforms the merely "natural" significance of ethics. Thus through its ethical effects, the reign of God is manifest in our history in non-definitive forms which keep on becoming obsolete. The ethical improvement of the world is *not* the reign of God (any more than the church is), but it is an anticipation of that reign.[65]

Again in Schillebeeckx's thought the ethics of the New Testament emerges as grounded in grace. So the formal question of ethics, "what must we do?" is transformed into the question, "in solidarity with God through and in Jesus Christ, what may we do?" Therefore, "for Chris-

---

[63]Ibid., p. 639.
[64]E. Schillebeeckx, *Jesus, op. cit.*, p. 58.
[65]E. Schillebeeckx, *Christ, op. cit.*, p. 599.

tians ethics is more something that is graciously allowed than something that is firmly compelled."[66] Christian ethics is not simply a prerequisite for the reign of God but the content of salvation. The ethical life that flows from grace is correlative with the life of the eschatological prophet.

Is such an ethic specifically Christian? For Schillebeeckx it is important to point out a necessary distinction between "Christianity" and the "specifically Christian."[67] Christianity as such is necessarily connected with human integrity and wholeness.[68] The "specifically Christian," on the other hand, has to do with the eschatological nature of Jesus' identity and the transforming nature of solidarity with and in him.

These positions on autonomous ethics were not without opposition. The adversaries to such positions proposed an "ethic of faith" and denounced the idea of restricting the influence of faith to motivation and horizons. Without faith, reason is unable to discover what is right or wrong. This position was accompanied by a depreciation of the human. It considered reason to be too weak to guarantee the certainty of norms; only faith could make good that deficiency.

Hans Urs von Balthasar is decisively a proponent of such an approach. He presented his position in an article entitled, "Nine Theses in Christian Ethics."[69] According to this author, Christian ethics springs forth from the person of Jesus Christ, who is the concrete and universal norm of all moral activity. "Jesus Christ is the concrete categorical imperative in the sense that he is not only a formal, universal norm of moral life, which can be applied to everyone, but also a concrete and personal norm."[70] In fact, "the concrete existence of Christ, his life, suffering, death, and bodily resurrection, takes up in itself, supplants and abrogates all other ethical systems."[71] This Christological perspective touches upon the role of natural law itself. "This natural law should not be divinized: rather it must retain its essentially relative character of referring

---

[66] Ibid., p. 587.

[67] Ibid., p. 765.

[68] Ibid., pp. 764–68.

[69] Hans Urs von Balthasar, "Nine Theses in Christian Ethics," *Homiletic and Pastoral Review*, (1976), pp. 9–22.

[70] Ibid., p. 13.

[71] Ibid., p. 13.

to the good."⁷² Christian ethics does not complement natural ethics, but challenges women and men to go beyond themselves. Natural ethics needs to admit the new revelation of God in Jesus Christ; it needs to accept all that the new law of Christ stands for and to delineate the ethical implications of that revelation. As far as Christianity is concerned, there is no valid anthropology except theocentric anthropology; and there is no valid ethics except a Christian ethics that begins, proceeds, and ends in fidelity to the revelation of God in Jesus Christ.

This Christocentric position is much closer to Protestant positions on natural law, and poses the necessity of a specific Christian ethic. The goal of human existence is not attainable without the revelation of Jesus Christ. The nature of revelation becomes crucial in this position; the theology of revelation becomes an important element in the debate on the nature of Christian ethics.

The Specificity of Christian Ethics from the Perspective of some American Roman Catholic Theologians

In the United States, within Roman Catholic circles, the debate on the specificity of Christian ethics was joined by Charles Curran. Curran underlined the basic relationship between human ethics and Christian ethics: "I maintain that the material content of moral theology or Christian ethics including concrete norms, attitudes, values and dispositions cannot claim to be unique. Non-Christians can and do share the same understanding and actions."⁷³ According to Curran, Christian ethics as an historically based science has a distinctive and exclusive source in the Scripture, tradition, and life of the Church. "Moral theology or Christian ethics is a thematic, reflexive, second order discourse which studies the way in which the Christian life should be lived. The Christian existence as members of the Christian community marks our whole existence and everything we do including our approach to morality."⁷⁴ Although the

---

⁷²Ibid., p. 21.

⁷³Charles E. Curran, "Horizons on Fundamental Moral Theology," *Horizons*, (1983), p. 9. Cf. Charles E. Curran, "Is There a Catholic and/or Christian Ethic?" *The Distinctiveness of Christian Ethics, op. cit.*, pp. 60–89.

⁷⁴Charles E. Curran, "Horizons on Fundamental Moral Theology," p. 9.

material content of Christian morality does not differ in principle from human morality, the way in which a Christian arrives at a moral decision is influenced by an explicit Christian understanding. By denying the existence of a specific Christian ethics, one is simply stating that those who have never heard of Jesus Christ can arrive at the same basic moral decisions, although they will arrive at those decisions by a different way than the Christian. Christians must understand themselves in the light of explicitly theological understandings shaped by revelation and symbols. Yet these are always mediated in and through the human. The theological premise from which Curran denies the existence of any specifically substantive content of morality is that of the universal salvific will of God.

Richard McCormick holds a similar position:

> My own view on the relation of Christian belief to *essential* ethics would be developed as follows. Since there is only one destiny possible to all men, there is existentially only one *essential* morality common to all men, Christians and non-Christians alike. Whatever is distinctive about Christian morality is found essentially in the style of life, the manner of accomplishing the moral tasks common to all persons, not in the tasks themselves. Christian morality is, in its concreteness and materiality, *human* morality. The theological study of morality accepts the human in all its fullness as its starting point. It is the *human* which is then illumined by the person, teaching and achievement of Jesus Christ. The experience of Jesus is regarded as normative because he is believed to have experienced what it is to be human in the fullest way and at the deepest level.[75]

There can be no contradiction, between the natural law and the evangelical law. The one does not surpass the other. There can be no opposition of Creation and Incarnation/Redemption. Jesus does not introduce another type of morality; he makes explicit that which is already implicit in creation. Therefore, in speaking of the ground of ethics one must speak of the common ground of ethics for all. This is true of essential and existential ethics. There is only one actual historical order, and in

---

[75] Richard McCormick, "Does Faith Add to Ethical Perception?", *The Distinctiveness of Christian Ethics, op. cit.*, p. 162.

that one order the human and Christian elements interact reciprocally. This is not to affirm that Christianity has no influence in ethical decisions. The influence is at the level of intentionality and motivation. McCormick writes:

> Therefore the specificity of Christian morality is found essentially in the very style of life, the manner of comporting oneself and of accomplishing the moral tasks which the Christian has in common with other men—a manner more dynamic, more assured, more joyous, more capable of following the example of Christ dying for men. For it is ultimately the law of the cross which remains the essentially Christian model of the manner of practicing the moral law . . . [76]

The major point made by contemporary American Roman Catholic authors who have based their positions on some aspects of Rahner's theology is that there is one single ground of ethics for Christians as for others. That one single ground of ethics is a creation that is already graced. What this implies is that God's grace is available and offered to all. In this perspective the Incarnation makes explicit what is already implicit in the order of a graced creation. The unity of the ground of ethics implies that there is only one ethical end for human existence. At the level of the ground of ethics, the morality of revelation is the morality of reason; faith in the revealed God in Jesus Christ and moral autonomy are not contradictory.

Within this perspective, revelation is, as Avery Dulles writes, "a transcendent fulfillment of the inner drive of the human spirit toward fuller consciousness."[77] God is not primarily revealed from outside but from within. Again, according to Dulles, "Revelation should not be understood as an insertion of fully articulated divine truths into the continuum of human knowledge, but rather as the process by which God, working within history and human tradition, enables his spiritual creatures to achieve a higher level of consciousness."[78] Scripture functions not as a source of information unattainable through reason, but as a reminder, as an exhortation. While the Scriptures are considered the pri-

---

[76] Ibid., p. 168.
[77] Avery Dulles, *Models of Revelation*, (New York: Doubleday, 1982), p. 98.
[78] Ibid., p. 100.

mary source of revelation, they are not understood simply as a quarry for revealed doctrine, for revelation is not simply an objective deposit. The Scriptures remain foundational texts, yet their canonicity is a result of a Church in the process of searching for its identity. This process is still going on, so that the Scriptures have to be read in a contemporary context and against the background of the tradition which the Scriptures relate for Christians. Paradigmatic events are in constant need of an interpretation, which is simultaneously critical and creative.

The position of these theologians can be understood as a mediating position, which emphasizes continuity between faith and reason. This approach is very well expressed by William May: "Christian ethics is continuous with the general moral strivings of mankind with respect to its principal concern and goal: how to make and keep human life human. It is distinctive in that it offers a specific perspective for assimilating the data and for integrating them into a vision of the meaning of human existence."[79] This mediating position represents an attempt at reinterpreting a natural law approach to ethics within a Christological perspective. It emphasizes the continuity of creation and redemptive Incarnation. It builds upon an anthropology in which men and women are understood as characterized by an openness to God's self-gift; an anthropology which emphasizes grace as operative within the human context. Humanity has one goal—God—and therefore one common morality. "Anonymous Christianity" is a necessary element of such an anthropology; without such a concept Christianity would be quite radically exclusive.

The various theologians we have surveyed up to now present us with a dialectical position on the specificity of Christian ethics. On the one hand, it is necessary to affirm that any moral norm necessary to achieve the goal of human existence must somehow be available to all. On the other hand, there is something specific to Christian ethics. This specificity lies in the realm of intentionality and its reference to Jesus Christ. These positions pose the never-resolved question of the relation of the particular and the universal. They also challenge Christianity to re-examine the foundation of its claim to absoluteness and uniqueness.

---

[79]William May, "Christian Ethics and the Human," *American Ecclesiastical Review*. 167 (1973), p. 683.

The concept of natural law plays an important role in this mediating position. Clearly the concept of a universal natural law has been the single and most continuous trademark of the traditional Roman Catholic understanding of morality.[80] While there is no one natural law tradition but many, it is the medieval concept which has had the most influence in shaping the traditional Roman Catholic understanding. This medieval understanding can be found most clearly delineated in the writings of Aquinas. For Aquinas, natural law is the possibility given to all human beings to participate in the eternal law whose source is a provident, omnipotent, and immutable God.

The medieval understanding provided a way of grounding, rationally, moral imperatives independent of divine revelation in Jesus Christ. Only God gives natural law. Therefore, natural law, for Aquinas, is like an ontological ground for all human laws and morality: it is the expression of God's self-consistency. Natural law functions at both the personal and the universal level. And while it is the basis of all human laws and morality, in no way does it dispense human beings from striving to understand what is required of them in particular situations. This understanding is derived from experience and inquiry. As Aquinas states, "What pertains to moral science is known through experience."[81] For Aquinas, the natural law represents a pattern of law as law: it is the logic of law itself. The word "nature" represents the dynamic aspect of the inner drive toward authentic humanness, i.e. it is a tendency rather than a code. As this concept of natural law found its way into the manuals of moral theology, it acquired a role it was not intended to have and took on a nonhistorical character divorced from any contact with biblical sources.

The theologians who propose a mediating position share a wariness of legalism relative to natural law. They vigorously reject the ahistorical nature of an understanding of natural law, which claims to provide tests of conduct appropriate to all human beings without regard for individual

---

[80] See Edward A. Malloy, "Natural Law Theory and Catholic Moral Theology," *American Ecclesiastical Review*, 169 (1975), pp. 456–469. Charles Curran (ed.,) *Absolutes in Moral Theology*, (New York: Corpus, 1968). C. B. Daly, *Natural Law Morality Today*, (London: Burns Oates, 1965). Yves Simon, *The Tradition of Natural Law: A Philosopher's Reflections*, (New York: Fordham University Press, 1965).

[81] Thomas Aquinas, *Summa*, Ia 2AE Q. 91, Art. 2.

peculiarities or the distinctiveness of historical situations.[82] These theologians share a resistance to the long emphasis in moral theology on norms grounded in unchanging human nature. Following in the footsteps of Fuchs,[83] they advocate a natural law based on Christian discipleship. In a more metaphysical idiom, the essential being of Christians from which their behavior or action is to flow is that of human beings who have been transformed into children of God. The traditional natural law understanding of morality must be reconsidered in light of this redemptive transformation of humankind.[84]

Within this framework, human reality is understood as involved in an eschatological tension between humanity transformed by God in Jesus Christ and the actual human condition, uncompleted and on the way. Underlying this eschatological understanding is an emphasis on freedom and futurity. Human nature is not static, complete, and self-enclosed; it is a task and a project. Within this anthropology, natural law can no longer be seen as a static, determined, a priori blueprint but, as Richard McCormick writes, as a "dynamically inviting possibility, a concrete project to be carried out in the midst of a concrete situation in which man's 'self' presents its demands to an ego conscientiously realizing itself. In other words, it is man's being charting his own becoming."[85]

---

[82]See Anthony Battaglia. *Toward a Reformulation of Natural Law* (New York: Seabury, 1981). Charles Curran, *Transition and Tradition in Moral Theology* (Notre Dame: Notre Dame University Press, 1979).

[83]Joseph Fuchs, *Natural Law: A Theological Investigation,* (New York: Sheed and Ward, 1965).

[84]See Enda McDonagh, *Doing the Truth: The Quest for Moral Theology,* (Notre Dame, Indiana: Notre Dame University Press, 1979), p. 34.

[85]Richard A. McCormick, "Human Significance and Christian Significance." In G. Outka and P. Ramsey, *Norm and Context* (New York: Scribner, 1968) p. 239.

II.

Protestant Positions.
The Question of Natural Law
and the Law of Christ

In the Acts of the Apostles 5:29 we read what is probably the first affirmation of the basic principle in Christian ethics, "we must obey God rather than men." In a variety of ways Christian ethics and especially Protestant ethics correlate moral decision with obedience to the command of God as revealed and expressed in the person of Jesus Christ. With Jesus Christ a new law is revealed; the relation of this law to the old law and to natural law becomes of crucial importance. According to James M. Gustafson, law "provides an illuminating subject matter for disclosing historic divergences between Catholic and Protestant ethics; its locus, authority, purpose, and religious significance open up more general issues."[1]

A form of Christocentrism is present at the very beginning of the Protestant Reformation, specifically in Luther's theology.[2] As such this focusing on the person of Christ and especially on the soteriological role Christ plays in the history of salvation led Luther and his followers to give less and less value to the role of natural law in the realm of morality. The power and efficacy of human reason to discover and establish what is morally right or wrong was incompatible with human sinfulness and

---

[1] James M. Gustafson, *Protestant and Roman Catholic Ethics* (Chicago: University of Chicago Press, 1978), p. 12.

[2] Marc Lienhart, *Luther: Witness to Jesus Christ*, tr. E.H. Robertson (Minneapolis: Augsburg, 1982).

the authority of Scripture as the unique source of the knowledge of good and evil. Insisting that there is no righteousness except in and through Christ, it was difficult for the Lutheran Reformers to accept that unconverted persons could perform good moral actions.[3]

In John Calvin we find a different approach. He emphasized the continuity between the law of nature, the law of the decalogue, and the new law. Calvin understood Jesus as *the* interpreter of the natural law and the decalogue but not as a giver of a new law. The Scriptures are necessary for an authentic reading of the natural law, for sin lessens reason's capacity in interpreting its own law.[4] The differences between the two Reformers' positions led to different emphases in later developments which are reflected by contemporary European Protestant theologians.

Karl Barth: Faith and Ethics

According to Karl Barth, any attempt to ground Christian ethics in human reason eliminates the paradox of God's revelation in Christ. The revelation of God in Jesus Christ is the sole condition of whatever knowledge we can have of God and of God's will for us. To gain insight into what God's will is, and therefore what is morally right and good, one needs to turn to Scripture. Ethics grounds itself in God's word; it does not need grounding from us.

It is Barth's Christocentrism more than his pessimistic view of human capacities which prevents him from accepting natural theology and natural law. For Barth, Jesus Christ's humanity becomes the norm of our

---

[3] "Luther's theological and religious context for the law and its uses alters the religious significance of morality and thus sets ethics in a different context. Fulfilling moral requirements leads not to salvation but to the presumption of righteousness before God. Orientation to one's proper natural end by a life of moral virtue and obedience to the law is a hazard to salvation and, given the state of corruption, not really possible in any case. Only out of fear is one moral. The antidote is proportionate to the poison; it is the free gift of imputed righteousness; salvation is by faith alone. Ethics as a subject of thought and writing has to be pursued within this theological and religious context." James Gustafson, *Protestant and Roman Catholic Ethics*, op. cit., p. 14.

[4] G. David Little, *Religion, Order and Law* (N.Y.: Harper and Row, 1969), Chap. 3 & 4.

humanity. All anthropological statements are based exclusively on the revelation of Christ.

For a Christian, an ethical action is always a grateful response to what God has done for us in Jesus Christ. To recognize what God has done for us in Christ, one must accept the sovereignty of God over one's action. This sovereignty expresses itself in the moral order in the form of commands. Such commands are not discovered by contemplating human nature but rather by hearing God's Word. The study of ethics is essentially theological. It is also essentially Christological because God's word is definitively manifested in Jesus Christ. "The obedience which the command of God demands of man is his decision for Jesus Christ. In each individual decision it is a special form, a repetition and confirmation of this decision."[5]

God's revelation in Jesus Christ is a revelation of truth and has universal validity. There is no humanity outside the humanity of Jesus Christ or the voluntary or involuntary glorifying of the grace of God which manifested itself in this humanity. There is no realization of the good which is not identical with the grace of Jesus Christ in its voluntary and involuntary confirmation. For there is no good which is not obedience to God's command.[6] There is some ontological relationship between Jesus Christ and all humankind. According to Gustafson:

> There is a functional equivalent in Barth's ethics to Rahner's concept of the anonymous Christian. Barth clearly eschews the concept of natural law for theological reasons; nonetheless, on his grounds it can be claimed that all ethics are theological or even Christian because all persons are elected to a relationship of grace through Christ, and this is their "essence." This is warranted by a biblical theology that accents the Christologies to which I have previously referred as well as by aspects of the tradition. All realization of the good is identical with the grace of Jesus Christ (not with "the moral law of nature"), and all moral commands are commands of the gospel, of grace. Thus those who are morally praiseworthy, it seems reasonable to conclude,

---

[5] Karl Barth, *Church Dogmatics II/2*, trans. by G. W. Bromiley and J. F. Torrance (Edinburgh: T. and T. Clark, 1957), p. 609.
[6] Ibid.

are implicitly Christian in the sense that they hear the command of grace even if they do not know it as grace.[7]

It is God's election of humanity in Jesus Christ that is the starting point of ethics. "Our contention is, however, that the dogmatics of the Christian Church, and basically the Christian doctrine of God, is ethics. This doctrine is, therefore, the answer to the ethical question, the supremely critical question concerning the good in and over every so-called good in human actions and modes of action."[8]

Moral norms receive their meaning only by reference to the "will of God" or the "command of God." Barth affirms that, "When we understand man from this point of view, we have a positive answer to give in regard to the goodness of his action, but we have to do it by pointing away from man to what God says, to God Himself. To put it concretely, we have to do it by pointing to God's commanding, to God as Commander."[9]

Within this perspective, the Scriptures are really the only source of moral knowledge for the Christian. "Even as ethics, theology is wholly and utterly the knowledge and representation of the Word and the work of God. What right conduct is for man is determined absolutely in the right conduct of God. It is determined in Jesus Christ."[10]

It is on the sources of ethics that Barth differs from Rahner and where his Christocentrism is most evident. For Rahner, while God's grace is essential in all realities, it always acts through nature and must have an impact on reality and therefore on morality. While for Rahner natural law itself is graced, for Barth there is a radical discontinuity between the truth of faith and that of human reason. God's commandment as revealed in Jesus is the starting point of an ethics that is specifically Christian. In Rahner the analogy of being is taken radically; it has a Christological depth. According to Rahner every intervention of God "is always only the becoming historical and becoming concrete of that 'intervention' in which God as the transcendental ground of the world has

---

[7] J. Gustafson, *Protestant and Roman Catholic Ethics*, op. cit., p. 123.
[8] K. Barth, *Church Dogmatics*, op. cit., p. 515.
[9] Ibid., p. 547.
[10] Ibid., pp. 537–38.

from the outset embedded himself in this world as its self-communicating ground."[11] Consequently, Rahner can perceive the Incarnation as "the unique and highest instance of the actualization of the essence of human reality."[12] God can be encountered everywhere; the quest for Christ can be initiated by anyone anywhere.

Barth replaces the *analogia entis* (analogy of being) with the *analogia fidei* (analogy of faith); the point of departure is always *from God*. Good and evil begin and end in the will of God. The autonomy of the world is merely apparent. The creature is to be strictly understood as a reality willed and created by God and distinct from God's own reality, that is to say, as the wonder of a reality, which by the power of God's love, has a place and persistence alongside of God's own reality. That being so, the continuity between God and the creature (the true *analogia entis*, by virtue of which God, the uncreated Spirit, can be revealed to the created spirit) cannot belong to the creature itself, but only to the Creator in relation to the creature.[13]

The presence of God as Spirit in our lives is never ontological; it is always eschatological.[14] This "presence as promise" is also true to God's presence in Jesus Christ. This perspective colors Barth's understanding of the role of revelation and Scripture in ethics. Revelation is not propositional, it is the living Word of God, Jesus Christ. The Bible bears witness to revelation but is not itself revelation; yet for Barth it is the fundamental and inspired medium through which the Church has access to the revealed Word. Scripture, for Barth, is revealed reality, a Christic reality. There is no fundamentalistic approach to Scripture; there is to revelation for it 'alone' establishes the humanity of all human persons. God's gracious and redemptive activity has its "center and goal" in Jesus Christ.

The authority of Scripture for Barth is understood in functional terms. As David Kelsey writes: "The texts are authoritative not in virtue of any inherent property they may have, such as being inerrant or in-

---

[11] Karl Rahner, *Foundations of Christian Faith*, (N.Y.: Crossroad, 1978), p. 87.
[12] Ibid., p. 218.
[13] Karl Barth, *The Holy Ghost and the Christian Life*, trans, R. Birch Hoyle (London: Frederick Mueller, 1938), p. 16.
[14] Ibid., p. 72.

spired, but in virtue of a function they fill in the life of the Christian community."[15] The Bible is not a revelation of an ethics but of the Living God, and thus its whole significance is that it points to God's call for faith and obedience. Revelation is centered on Jesus Christ. Fundamental to Barth's position is a clear distinction between revelation which is understood as divine action, and religion which is simply a human activity. It is Barth's contention that revelation has become a reality in Christ and nowhere else. This is clearly affirmed at the beginning of the second half of the first volume of *Church Dogmatics*. "According to the Holy Scripture God's revelation takes place in that God's Word became a man and that this man has become God's Word. The incarnation of the eternal Word, Jesus Christ, is God's revelation."[16] All attempts on the part of women and men to know God outside of Jesus Christ are useless. God's activity in Christ absorbs and in a sense negates all human activity. Humankind can know nothing about God except what God has revealed about himself—there are no innate capacities. Men and women have no innate capacities to experience the divine; all capacities are given to them by the Word itself. Religion is perceived by Barth as humanity's attempt to do what only Christ can do: reveal and please God.[17] As such, religion and religions are totally opposed to Christ and his revelation.[18]

Barth's position on the specificity of Christian ethics is essentially dialectical. It does not easily fit any of the classical Protestant positions nor does it easily co-exist with contemporary ones. Ethics is Christian ultimately because of God's graciousness. Jesus Christ is the revelation because he is the grace of God made manifest to us—grace in the full sense of the conception.[19] For Barth, if God were not gracious, if God did not of his own free decision turn toward women and men there would be no revelation."[20]

---

[15] David H. Kelsey, *The Uses of Scripture in Recent Theology* (Philadelphia: Fortress Press, 1975), p. 47.

[16] Karl Barth, *Church Dogmatics I/2* (Edinburgh: T. and T. Clark 1956) p. 1.

[17] Ibid., p. 329.

[18] Ibid., p. 320-35.

[19] Cf. K. Barth, *Church Dogmatics* IV/3 (Edinburgh: T. and T. Clark, 1961) p. 97 and K. Barth, *The Humanity of God*, Trans. T. Weiser (Richmond: John Knox Pres, 1960).

[20] Ibid.

Ethical positions are justified without reference to a universal ground of rationality outside the internal logic of God's gracious revelation in Jesus Christ. The normativeness of any ethical claim is established by tracing back from it to an understanding of how its content refers to that gracious being revealed in the person of Jesus Christ.[21]

Emil Brunner

While Karl Barth followed his own path, Emil Brunner, a contemporary, was attempting his own interpretation of the Protestant tradition. Brunner shares Barth's emphasis on the commandment of God as the beginning point for Christian ethics. Where he differs considerably from Barth is in the fact that he sees this commandment as embodied in the very fabric of common human existence, in what is referred to as the "orders of creation." God's will becomes visible in the structures of God's creation and as such is available to all who seek it.

The possible corruption of such "orders of creation" is no reason to deny God's causal relation to them. According to Brunner there is a link between God's commandment and concrete historical situations. God's commandment is encountered in the

> general laws of creation, of the preservation and furtherance of life, and of specifically human life and in those existing facts of human corporate life which lie at the root of all historical life and may vary, but are unalterable in their fundamental structure and at the same time, relate and unite men to one another in a definite way.[22]

One response can be a response to God's call, obedience to God's commandment. "Only through the perception of this truth is the ascetic con-

---

[21] "God's self-interpretation [revelation] is interpretation as correspondence. Let it be well noted: **as** his own **interpreter** God corresponds to his own being. Since, however, God as his own interpreter (also in his external works) **is** he himself, since also in this happening as such it is a question of the **being** of God, then the highest and last statement which can be made about the being of God is: God corresponds to himself." Eberhard Jungel, *The Doctrine of the Trinity: God Is In Becoming* (Grand Rapids: Eerdmans, 1976), pp. 23–24.

[22] Emil Brunner, *The Divine Imperative*, trans. Olive Wyon (Philadelphia: Westminster Press, 1947) p. 210.

ception of life completely eliminated; at the same time this truth eliminates all mere 'secularism' of outlook. One who, in faith, dwells within these orders, and renders service through them while he is working in *the world,* is also working in the *Kingdom of God.*"[23]

Since creation does not exist simply for its own sake but is intended for perfection, our responsiveness to God's creation involves a critical cooperation. Adaptation to the existing order, therefore, because that order has been created by God, is the first point in the Christian ethic; but it is never the last point. The first priority is always what God wills as Creator; but—even apart from the extra significance given it as a result of our sin—it is not the last. For God wills to lead the creation out beyond itself, into the perfecting of all things. God does not preserve the world simply in order to preserve it, but in order that it may be brought to perfection.

The will of God must be made intelligible in human terms; God's freedom must be expressed in order, if God's action is to have any intelligibility at all. That intelligibility is perceivable by humankind apart from revelation—humanity has a God-given capacity to understand God's word, for human reason is the point of encounter between humanity and God. While reason cannot give answers (since only revelation can do this), it does prepare the way for God's Word. It is on this point that Brunner differs from Barth, for whom there is no human capacity to hear the Word; the Word creates its own capacity.[24]

Brunner affirms the specificity of Christian ethics differently than Barth because of the value the former places on reason and on the "orders of creation." His position is clearly not that of Rahner, yet there is a point of rapprochement with Rahner which is not present in Barth. Brunner sought in the "orders of creation" a reality that endures across times and cultures, that establishes a bridge to those not sharing the Christian faith. Basically then, Christian ethics for Brunner "is more than, but not other than, the functional requirements of a society in which human life can flourish. So understood, Brunner and Bonhoeffer converge with the main current of modern Roman Catholic thought on natural law."[25]

---

[23]Ibid., p. 337.
[24]Ibid., p. 214.
[25]R. Lovin, *Christian Faith and Public Choices,* op. cit., p. 161.

For Brunner, Christian morality is a matter of response to God's will as made known in Jesus Christ through the authority of the Holy Spirit. A command from God is heard in each situation with a compelling clarity by the person of faith. Faith is therefore central, for the will of God, as revealed in Jesus Christ, cannot be known apart from the situation of faith. No general moral principle can simply encompass God's will. Faith makes the believer into a new being with new capacities for response.

Brunner shares with Karl Barth and other continental Protestant theologians the conviction that God's will is totally free, and confronts men and women in the person of Jesus Christ with an imperative which demands obedient response. The obedient person has no standards apart from his/her openness to God's will as revealed in the person of Jesus Christ. There is really no Christian ethic unless God has made possible such obedience; and this God has done in the person of Jesus Christ.

A Theocentric Approach to Christian Ethics: The Thought of James M. Gustafson

The mediating position of some influential American Roman Catholic theologians, while radically different from the European Roman Catholic and conservative Protestant positions, are considerably influenced by the writings of Rahner and Fuchs. However these positions have not advanced the debate; they have basically made the same points. On the other hand in the American Protestant positions such as those of James Gustafson and Stanley Hauerwas, we find a continuity with earlier European positions but with new emphases and directions.[26] In a series of well-chosen questions, James Gustafson outlined the various problems inherent in the specificity of Christian ethics.[27] What philosophical foundations are necessary and sufficient so that theological ethics can do justice both to the historical particularities of the Christian tradition and

---

[26]Gustafson has dealt with this question in a variety of different books. His position is expressed in his *Can Ethics Be Christian?*, (Chicago, University of Chicago Press, 1975) and in "Can Ethics Be Christian? Some Conclusions" in *The Distinctiveness of Christian Ethics,* ed. C. Curran and R. McCormick, op. cit., p. 146–155.

[27]J. Gustafson, "Can Ethics Be Christian? Some Conclusions," in *The Distinctiveness of Christian Ethics,* ed. C. Curran and R. McCormick, op. cit., pp. 146–155.

to the common humanity and rationality that religious persons share with all members of our species? What foundations are necessary and sufficient so that theological ethics can do justice to both the persistent temporal continuities of human experience (nature) and the historical changes in it (history)? What foundations are necessary and sufficient so that theological ethics can do justice to both the dimensions of human freedom and individual personal existence on the one hand and the limitations of freedom and co-humanity on the other?[28]

According to James Gustafson the question about the specificity of Christian ethics depends on what one means by ethics. Ethics as such must be universal and cannot be restrictive. The foundation of ethics must be reason and not religion. The morality of the Christian community, or for that matter of any other religious community, falls into the domain of ethics inasmuch as its justifying principle is "rationally" definable. If the justifying principle were "religious," such a morality would be excluded from ethics. Yet an ethical act can be done for a variety of motives. While religion and therefore Christianity is grounded primarily on an experience of God, and not on ethical considerations, it can powerfully motivate an ethical decision. While the morally good and the theologically good cannot be collapsed into one, one can be qualified by the other. That qualification can be quite formal.[29] At the heart of the Christian faith is the experience of God in the person of Christ. That experience leads to specific moral actions. One is not religious in order to be moral, but being Christian (or religious) does lead to moral actions. "It is intelligible to speak of morality, and by derivation of ethics, as Christian in the sense that Christianity offers reasons for morality itself and reasons for persons to be moral."[30]

Such a morality by nature implies a starting point that is particular and historical. Gustafson is committed to the historical point of view and to an empirical grounding for ethics. Human beings are not capable of developing an ideal moral theory, or formulating an ethical theory which disregards the implications of human moral agency, of the individual's involvement in a particular culture, location and involvement in society,

---

[28] J. Gustafson, "Can Ethics Be Christian? Some Conclusions" in *The Distinctiveness of Christian Ethics*, op. cit., p. 151.
[29] Ibid., p. 150.
[30] Ibid., p. 150.

and interdependence in the ordering of the natural world. Any such efforts to develop ideal moral theories assume a posture of spectator which is not finally possible or justifiable, though one appreciates their intellectual brilliance and learns from them. Indeed, as sociologists of knowledge and some philosophers, theologians, and intellectual historians have pointed out, such efforts are themselves part of a cultural tradition; they have their own intellectual history.[31]

Gustafson is particularly aware that the cultural context conditions visions and ways of life. These latter

> grow out of aspects of cultural histories and societies, and can be sustained only in communities that have their distinctive symbols, languages, and rites. This is true not only of religious views and activities, but it is necessarily true of them. Communities are bound together by common interest, common loyalties, common standards, and common languages. If a community of autonomous rational moral agents, that fictive denomination into which many contemporary moral philosophers seek to convert us all, were actualized, it too would share these characteristics.[32]

Morality, and specifically religious morality, is socially embodied, "ecclesially" determined. The sustaining of a theological interpretation of humanity must take place in the context of a religious community, with its first-order religious language, its liturgies and symbols, and its procedures for transmitting a heritage. As the author writes,

> the distinctive aspects of the views developed in this book are not completely at home in any particular Christian denomination, liturgy, or community. Yet they are grounded in some aspects of the rich and varied heritage of the Bible and of the Christian Church and tradition. There are themes in the worship and religious life of the Christian tradition that do evoke and sustain the views I have espoused. In emphasizing some of them I am not merely attaching an idiosyncratic

---

[31] Ibid.
[32] *Ethics From a Theocentric Perspective, Theology and Ethics,* Vol. 1, (Chicago: University of Chicago Press, 1981), p. 317.

view onto a tradition; I am indicating various aspects of the tradition that evoke and sustain my views.[33]

While community is essential, it is also historical and therefore relative. Gustafson emphasizes the church as a natural community in order to

> show that the historical and social relativity of the Church is part of its essential character. This is so in a double sense. This relativity is of the essence of its nature as an historical community, and it is essential to the achievement of its purpose in the world. The Church is earthen—of the stuff of natural and historical life. The Church is a vessel, it is useful. The contact with man and culture is made through the social and historical media of the church—its natural functions, political forms, etc.[34]

While Gustafson is determined to begin his ethics from a historical and social starting point, he is nonetheless interested in arriving at some universal perspective.

> To strive for the universal is not only intellectually valiant but also a necessary motivation in theological work. It is necessary for apologetic purposes; the intelligibility of the particular can be made clear and to some extent more persuasive by demonstrating that its insights and truths refer to the experiences of many if not all persons and that its justifications can be made clear in non-esoteric language. It is also necessary for purposes of internal criticism of a historical tradition. By such means, blind spots can be indicated, for instance, places where false or inadequate assumptions have been revealed, assumptions which were made in the tradition about such things as the ordering of the natural world, the motivations of human behavior, and the reliability and historical accuracy of critical texts. The shifting within a tradition occurs in part by exposing it to light which comes from relevant knowledge and to ideas from other movements of thought. Undue parochialism becomes clear. Where historic partic-

---

[33] J. Gustafson, *Treasure in Earthen Vessels: The Church as a Human Community* (N.Y.: Harper and Brothers, 1961) p. X.
[34] Ibid.

ularity is adduced as support for ideas which are no longer viable or are marginal to the importance of what the tradition stands for, it can be eliminated.[35]

> Ethics must begin from within a specific tradition and attempt to establish a universal significance. This process must necessarily determine the nature of Christian ethics.
>
> The central issue is that Christianity has always claimed its historical particularity—the biblical events and their record—to have universal significance and import.[36]

Certainly a substantive enterprise in theology from biblical times forward has been to overcome and sustain that particularity while nonetheless insisting that its significance is universal.

Within these perspectives, Gustafson's position on the distinctiveness of Christian ethics must necessarily be complex. He attempts to avoid what he sees as two extremes: that Christian principles are always defensible on rational moral grounds, and that Christian faith involves a specific and exclusive way of being human. The author does not want to divide radically the order of creation and that of faith.[37]

That medium "through which God's universal purposes for humankind and the rest of creation are experienced with compelling clarity" is the person of Jesus Christ. Gustafson underlines in a variety of ways and in a variety of places that in Jesus God is revealed "with compelling clarity," and that revelation qualifies the morality of the Christian. The experience of God in the person of Jesus Christ engenders and requires specific characteristics in moral agents.[38] As Gus-

---

[35] James Gustafson, *Ethics from a Theocentric Perspective*, Vol. I, op. cit., p. 151.
[36] Ibid, p. 68.
[37] J. Gustafson, *Can Ethics Be Christian?*, op. cit., p. 168.
[38] The crucial point is that the media through which God's universal purposes for men and creation are experienced with compelling clarity take on a special authority for those who share the experience. That authority does not lead to a whole unique set of moral values and principles for Christians, but there are certain principles and values that can be rationally inferred from the historically particular media that might direct action in a distinctive way. J. Gustafson, "Can Ethics Be Christian? Some Conclusions," in *The Distinctiveness of Christian Ethics*, op. cit., p. 151–152.

tafson writes, it is important to ask within the Christian context: "If one experiences God's reality, particularly informed by the Christian story, what sort of moral person ought one to become?" "What intentions and dispositions ought to be characteristic of Christians?" For Gustafson, the "Christian story" has a compelling clarity and therefore has a powerful value in grounding moral action. Yet this story does not "guarantee that the actions of Christians are 'morally better' than the actions of others whose principles and values are derived from 'purely rational' bases."[39] Yet the Christian story, the revelation in Christ, leads people to "apprehend God" with compelling clarity, and from that apprehension a fidelity to God follows which gives distinctive though not exclusive authority to the media through which that experience occurs.

Christian ethics is related to Christian experience; it is for Christians. Extra-Christians can make authentic moral decisions and live superior lives without the help of Christian ethics. Yet for Christians Christ is a norm and a source of ethics, and according to Gustafson, this norm, this source, can have a universal value. The author approaches this perspective in a similar way to that of Rahner. Apart from explicit faith, Christ's relevance to other religious traditions cannot be grasped. Yet a Christian can affirm that all—Christians, Muslims, and unbelievers— "exist within the Kingship of Christ or the election of humanity in Christ."[40]

This position clearly resonates with the "anonymous Christian approach." What "anonymous Christianity" means is that Christ and Christianity are, from one perspective, the manifestation of a possibility that is in principle present everywhere, and, from another perspective, the instrument through which that universal possibility can be manifested and known.

For Gustafson, belief in Jesus Christ can and does lead to specific ethical decisions. One can be moral for "religious" reasons; morality can be grounded in theological beliefs. What is specific about such grounding for Christians is the person of Jesus Christ.[41]

---

[39]Ibid., p. 153.

[40]J. Gustafson, *Christ and the Moral Life*, (New York: Harper and Row, 1968), 54.

[41]"If morality is qualified by religion in this sense, then Christian ethics is possible

For Gustafson, it is necessary to draw moral inferences from Christian beliefs. That process occurs in the lived experience of communities. Yet as the author writes: "The moral principles and values inferred from beliefs guide human actions but do not provide absolute certitude that these actions are perfectly in accord with God's purpose."[42] Yet there is confidence, though not blind trust, that these historically particular media are a trustworthy basis for founding moral values and principles that are in accord with God's will and reality. The "Christian way" implies ethical principles that are specific and distinctive; in some cases these same principles may be universalized. Yet "Christian morality" is not simply grounded in reason, but in the experience of God as revealed and proclaimed in the person of Jesus Christ.[43]

What is inferred from a particular set of beliefs and communal experience may be of universal value. Yet the Christians do not have "an epistemological privilege that enables them to articulate the principles of ultimate reality, of the being of God, with such objectivity that all persons should be persuaded on rational grounds."[44] There is a need for "experiential confirmation" and for those who have had such an "experiential confirmation" there are particular and distinctive obligations.[45]

---

in two aspects. One is making clear the morphology of Christian experience of being moral for 'religious' reasons. The second is to develop action-guiding principles and values that can be inferred from these reasons; the ethical task is to answer the question, 'If one is moral for these reasons, what sort of moral action ought one to do?' 'What values and principles guide the discernment of what God is enabling and requiring me (us) to do?' Theology not only provides 'ultimate grounds' for morality; the morality that it grounds is qualified by the theological beliefs. Christian beliefs do not only ground morality; since the reality of God has compelling clarity through Jesus, the morality that it grounds is qualified by that medium. Thus inferences of principles and values, and the ordering of priority of them, are qualified by him." J. Gustafson, "Can Ethics Be Christian? Some Conclusions," in *The Distinctiveness of Christian Ethics,* op. cit. 158.

[42]Ibid., p. 153.

[43]"Christian ethics is the intellectual discipline that renders an account of this experience and that draws the normative inferences from it for the conduct of the Christian community and its members. The practical impact is to aid the community and its members in discerning what God is enabling and requiring them to be and to do." J. Gustafson, *Can Ethics Be Christian?,* op. cit. 165.

[44]J. Gustafson, *Can Ethics Be Christian?,* op. cit., p. 165.

[45]The author writes: "If, however, distinctive obligations follow from a 'way of life'

Gustafson's position, while emphasizing the mediating role of Jesus Christ, is clearly not Christocentric. The importance of Jesus Christ for our self-understanding and for our relationship to God is relative. Although Gustafson affirms that in Jesus the Christ "God is made compellingly clear," he does not have an understanding of Revelation that could ground such an affirmation. In relation to the use of biblical materials in ethics, Gustafson writes:

> For Barth we have knowledge of God only because God has chosen to reveal himself to man. And God has chosen to reveal himself in the life and events of a particular people, and in Jesus Christ. Thus the biblical record and materials are the source of God's revelation, and thus of any reliable knowledge of God. I deliberately refrained from using the term "revelation" to characterize how humans become informed about God on the grounds that what is called revelation is reflection on human experiences in the face of the ultimate power and powers. The biblical records, in such a view, are an account of great importance, but not the exclusive source of our understanding of God. The term revelation could be used within the framework of my discussion only in a very weak sense, if at all.[46]

This concept of Revelation gives a great deal of importance to human experience as such. Thus the author can claim that:

> questions of ethics, Christian or any other, can be established on the basis of both general human experience and reflection on literature in the field. . . . It [his method] assumes that one can properly evaluate writings in theological ethics from other criteria than those established in and by revelation. When a constructive proposal is made in

---

to which one is committed, then these are moral obligations to moral principles that follow from a distinctively Christian experience and way of life. The choice of that way of life is not purely arbitrary, that is, totally irrational. One can give reasons for believing what Christians believe, though they will not be fully persuasive to those for whom these beliefs are not confirmed experientially. I am increasingly persuaded that no other definable 'ways of life' including the most 'rationally defensible' ones, and those that require the greatest rational disinterestedness to pursue, are exempt from some sort of confirmation in the experience of adherents." *Can Ethics Be Christian?*, op. cit. p. 165–166.

[46]J. Gustafson, *Ethics From a From a Theocentric Perspective*, in Vol. 2 *Ethics and Theology* (Chicago: University of Chicago Press, 1984), p. 28.

the last chapter, the key terms used are not drawn from revelation, or even theological literature. This is done out of the conviction that any significance of the work of Christ for the moral life takes place through such aspects of selfhood as disposition, intention, and judgment that are common to all men. Thus some of the points used in the critical analysis in the end become normative in my attempts to make constructive Christian ethical proposals.[47]

The interpretation of God's intentions and purposes is developed and discerned through events of human history and experience. To appeal to revelation as a "private source of knowledge" is a dangerous process.[48] The Christian community as such cannot isolate itself from the person of Jesus as presented to us in the Scriptures. " . . . in the person and accounts of Jesus, who marks the particular historic identity of this community, there are poignant exemplifications in his life, activity, teachings, and death of what theocentric piety and fidelity call upon us to do."[49] Yet awareness of this reality "is not achieved simply by looking to the biblical material to see what it claims God has commanded."[50]

According to Gustafson, ethics as such cannot be specifically anything else but human. But specific groups of human beings can be motivated to ethical decisions in a variety of ways, religion being one of those ways. Such a motivation as religion, even the Christian religion, is not privileged with any special "supernatural" characteristics; the ultimate test of its effectiveness is the result: what kind of moral agents does it foster?

There is clearly an empirical emphasis in Gustafson's position as mentioned above. This emphasis is accompanied by a desire to move from the particular of the Christian tradition to the universal of human existence. According to the author, the first task of theological ethics is to establish convictions about God and God's relations to the world. To make a case for how some things really and ultimately are is the first task of theological ethics. What the theologian writes about ethics must rea-

---

[47] J. Gustafson, *Christ and the Moral Life,* op. cit. 9–10.
[48] Cf. J. Gustafson, *Ethics from a Theocentric Perspective,* Vol. 2, op. cit., p. 7.
[49] Ibid., p. 319.
[50] Ibid.

sonably follow from these convictions. To be sure, it is impossible to have a philosophical theology, or a metaphysics, or a cosmology, based on "reason alone" from which follow ethics based on reason alone. "In some respects (with qualifications made in volume 1) my work is more in accord with that intention than it is with a view that takes biblical 'revelation' as the exclusive basis for theological ethics."[51] "Convictions about God and God's relations to the world" are to be found within the Christian tradition, but also within the larger human community. While such convictions may not involve the person of Jesus Christ, they will reveal "particular potentialities and values to human life and thus that human beings have an accountability for the ordering of life, and a distinctive value within it."[52] There is a certain "form of the human which gives us knowledge of the essence of the human."[53] There are universals within the human realm so that one must assume continuities of experience which presuppose that humanity has a nature as well as a history. One cannot dispose of such continuities by appealing to the authority of Scripture as the source of the proper understanding of reality. Other evidences and arguments than scriptural ones are required to settle issues as complex as this.[54] These continuities are God-given and so it is the function of theological ethics to discern these continuities in order to grasp what human reality is capable of as authentic moral agent.[55]

What kind of theology and Christology lies behind Gustafson's position? Gustafson clearly moves away from any form of Christocentrism. Revelation of God in Jesus Christ is not understood as having ultimate status. Writing about his ethics Gustafson affirms, "It is probably 'theo-

---

[51] Ibid., p. 98.

[52] Ibid., p. 56.

[53] Ibid., p. 55.

[54] J. Gustafson, *Theology and Christian Ethics* (Philadelphia: Pilgrim Press, 1974) 189–190.

[55] [For] "God orders the life of the world through the patterns and processes of interdependence in which human persons, institutions, communities, and the species participate. These patterns and processes are a basis, foundation, or ground for human ends and values and for moral principles. They are fundamentally necessary conditions which have to be met for other values and ends to be fulfilled. They are not a sufficient basis of ethics; specific ends and moral principles are not simply deduced from them. But they are a necessary basis for ethics; the oughtness of ends and principles is grounded in, or based upon, their isness." J. Gustafson, *Ethics From a Theocentric Perspective*, Vol. 2, op. cit., 298.

centric and pious enough but in a general or cosmic sense,' and not decisively related to Jesus Christ. It might be considered 'merely theocentric,' and thus not sufficiently an ethic 'about' Jesus.''[56] In Jesus there are poignant exemplifications in his life, activity, teachings, and death of what theocentric piety and fidelity call upon us to do. God is perceived as one who is beyond human control. "He is the sovereign power and our destiny and the destiny of the worlds are not in our hands."[57]

The Christian God is one who cannot be manipulated; nor can the creation God has brought about. What is said of God can somehow be said of "the divine ordering of things." This "objectification of God" makes it difficult to understand many of the Christian symbols that relate to God as a loving and provident father/mother. It is not accidental that Gustafson rejects the doctrine of an afterlife. As Lisa Cahill writes:

> It is no oversight that causes Gustafson to describe the significance of Jesus in terms of resignation to his cross, with no counterpoint of resurrection promise and fulfillment. The eschatological symbols of the New Testament are rejected in favor of an interpretation of Jesus in terms of struggle, suffering, doubt, and final consent to the inevitable, even when not perceived as a human good.[58]

The Resurrection plays no real role in Gustafson's perspective. While Gustafson affirms that "Christology is the most critical doctrinal issue for any Christian theology,"[59] yet it plays very little role since ultimately too much emphasis on the Incarnation not only leads to a false Christocentrism but to an anthropocentrism that Gustafson sees as a serious deviation. Human beings are not the center and crown of the universe but only one part of a much broader reality.

Paul Ramsey

While J. M. Gustafson is the one American Protestant theologian who has most specifically addressed the question of the specificity of

---

[56] Ibid., p. 87.
[57] Ibid., p. 320.
[58] Lisa Cahill, "Consent in Time of Affliction: The Ethics of a Circumspect Theist," *The Journal of Religious Ethics*, Vol. 13/1, 1985, p. 33.
[59] J. Gustafson, *Ethics from a Theocentric Perspective*, Vol. 1, op. cit., p. 275.

Christian ethics, there are a number of strands in contemporary American Protestant Christian ethics. Paul Ramsey has been for almost two decades a steadfast proponent of the Christian ethics of love. This ethics is not left on a level of general principles, but applied to specific cases and situations.[60]

His ethics is clearly more confessional than that of Gustafson, and is more clearly based on the Bible. He writes,

> As a treatise on basic Christian ethics, this book endeavors to stand within the way the Bible views morality. The central ethical notion or "category" in Christian ethics is "obedient love"—the sort of love the gospels describe as "love fulfilling the law" and St. Paul designates as "faith that works through love."[61]

Ramsey sees the Bible as authoritative for ethics and simultaneously emphasizes the centrality of Christ. Basic to his position are the following affirmations:

> Christian ethics stands . . . in decisive relation to Jesus Christ . . . As a consequence, Christocentric ethics contrasts both with humanism's cutting the pattern to fit man and also with any religious or mystical ethics which may indeed be theocentric and pious enough but in a general or cosmic sense not historically related to this particular man, Jesus Christ. Christian ethics necessarily means a religious ethics "about" Jesus irreducible to the so-called "simple" religious ethics "of" Jesus. The Christian, indeed, is consistently more Christocentric, considerably less merely theocentric, in religious and ethical outlook than was Jesus himself.[62]

---

[60] Paul Ramsey, *Basic Christian Ethics* (N.Y.: Scribner's, 1950) p. XI. For evaluations of Ramsey's works, see James T. Johnson and David H. Smith, eds., *Love and Society: Essays in the Ethics of Paul Ramsey* (Missoula, Mont: Scholars Press, 1974). The essays by David H. Smith, Donald Evans, Charles E. Curran, Paul R. Camenish, and David Little are all critical analyses. See also Charles E. Curran, *Politics and Christian Ethics: A Dialogue with Paul Ramsey* (Philadelphia: Fortress, 1973).

[61] Paul Ramsey, *The Patient as Person* (New Haven: Yale University Press, 1970) p. XII.

[62] Ibid.

Stanley Hauerwas and Christian Ethics[63]

According to this author what is needed in Protestant theological ethics is a return to the language of character and virtue. By character he means "the qualifications of man's self-agency through his beliefs, intentions and actions, by which man acquires a moral history befitting his self-determining nature."[64]

Ethics is done from the perspective of the moral agent's continuities of self-hood. Within the Christian context the focus must be on the distinctive story of Jesus. In fact, for Hauerwas, stories are the crucial element in Christian ethics. Whatever unity is needed in order to avoid personal and ethical fragmentation will not come from a priori norms, or abstract systems of thought, but from a specific story, that of Jesus Christ, and of the community of believers. Faith in Jesus involves the reconstruction of an individual's identity in light of the community's story.[65] Narratives are essential for our understanding of God, the self, and the world.

It is within the perspective of narrative that the distinctiveness of Christian ethics can be perceived.

> Christian ethics is, therefore, not an ethic based on universal presuppositions that can be known separate from these (the Christian community's) particular peoples' traditions. Rather, Christian ethics is

---

[63] Stanley Hauerwas, *A Story Shaped Society: Toward a Constructive Christian Social Ethic* (Notre Dame: University of Notre Dame Press, 1980). *A Community of Character Toward a Constructive Christian Social Ethic* (Notre Dame: University of Notre Dame Press, 1981). *Truthfulness and Tragedy: Further Investigations in Christian Ethics* (Notre Dame: University of Notre Dame Press, 1977). *Character and the Christian Life: A Study in Theological Ethics* (San Antonio: Trinity University Press, 1975).

[64] S. Hauerwas, *Character and the Christian Life*, op. cit., p. 11.

[65] G.W. Stroup, *The Promise of the Narrative. Theology Recovering the Gospel in the Church*, (Atlanta: John Knox Press, 1981). John Shea, *Stories of God*, (Chicago: St. Thomas More, 1978). Gene Outka, "Character, Vision, and Narrative," in *Religious Studies Review*, 6/2 (1980).

the discipline that attempts to remind us of the kinds of skills, linguistic, conceptual, and practical, that are necessary to be such a people and to place ourselves faithfully within that story for it is not enough that we know that story, we must learn to live it through our hands and feet.[66]

The skill involved in learning the story and living it is called tradition. This tradition is the Christian tradition. "As Christians we maintain that the benchmark of that appropriation is to be found in our faithfulness to the life and death of Jesus Christ. Thus, morally central to Christian ethics is faithfulness to this man as a guide for our appropriation of God's story as our own."[67]

The moral life of the Christians is claimed to be specific because it is shaped by a specific story. It is not in the decision of individual Christians that the specificity of the moral life is apparent, but in that which is enduring and continuous. What endures and is on-going from situation to situation, from context to context, is the narrative.

The normative nature of the virtues necessary to one's character cannot be deduced a priori, but needs to be seen in light of the story of Jesus as found in the Scriptures. The Scriptures as such have normative value because they are the call to discipleship; they also help us remember the story of God for the continual guidance of our community and individual lives.[68]

The Scriptures have authority within the ecclesial community; the only place where a Christian way of life is possible is within an ecclesial community. What is distinctive about Christian ethics is that it emerges from within a specific community, the Christian community. What is distinctive about this community is the story of Jesus of Nazareth.

This story defines the community: the life of the community, eschatologically taken, is the basic test for the truthfulness of the story. The particularity of Christian ethics does not lead to a form of relativism nor to the questionability of its truth. According to Hauerwas, the task of the Christian is not to defeat relativism by argument, but rather to

---

[66]S. Hauerwas, "The Demands of a Truthful Story: Ethics and the Pastoral Task," *Chicago Studies*, 21 (1982): 64–65.

[67]S. Hauerwas, *A Community of Character*, op cit., p. 66.

[68]Ibid.

witness to a God who requires confrontation. To be a witness is different than being a philosopher—the call to be a witness is not grounded on the assumption that one possesses an absolute truth that others have implicitly and need to be made aware of. The call to be a witness is based on the understanding that truth is arrived at only by confrontation with the truth. Approaching Christian ethics through narrative, according to Hauerwas, is "an attempt to do constructive Christian theology and ethics in a nonreductionistic manner so that questions of truth may be rightly asked."[69] The truthfulness of the narratives can be tested in the interrelation of narrative and character. The author writes:

> Significant narratives produce significant and various characters necessary for the understanding and richness of the story itself. Just as scientific theories are partially judged by the fruitfulness of the activities they generate, so narratives can and should be judged by the richness of moral character and activity they generate. Or just as significant works of art occasion a tradition of interpretation and criticism, so significant narratives are at once the result of a continuation of moral communities and character that form nothing less than a tradition. And without tradition we have no means to ask questions of truth and falsity.[70]

The truth of the Christian narratives becomes a matter of the kind of life lived in relation to them. "The emphasis on narrative as the grammar of religious convictions is an attempt to locate the question of the truthfulness of religious convictions without losing the insistence that the moral force of those claims is essential for their truthfulness."[71]

Conclusion

The Roman Catholic positions on the specificity of Christian ethics represent a mediating perspective, an attempt at reinterpreting a natural law approach to ethics within a christological perspective. They emphasize the continuity of creation and redemptive Incarnation and locate the specificity of Christian ethics within the realm of the intentional.

---

[69] Ibid.
[70] Ibid.
[71] Ibid., p. 30.

While the Protestant positions we have seen are specifically christological, they are formally theocentric. What is important is the will of God for us, God's being for us. So an important issue for all of these positions is whether God can be understood as a historical agent who comes to us graciously and redemptively in the person of Jesus Christ. This understanding can occur only in the ecclesial community. Since this ecclesial community is the result of God's activity, it is closely related to the biblical drama and is concerned to proclaim the mighty acts of God as expressed in both covenants. The specificity of Christian ethics is intrinsically linked to its ecclesial nature. It is on the role of the ecclesial community in ethics that Roman Catholic positions differ from Protestant ones.

III.

Christian Ethics and the Ecclesial Community

Introduction

Our survey of Protestant and Roman Catholic positions on the specificity of Christian ethics reveals elements of similarity and also of diversity. It is my hope that getting at the reasons for those dissimilarities will clarify the question of the specificity of Christian ethics. There is no neat way to explain the dissimilarities that exist within the various Roman Catholic positions and within the Protestant positions, nor between the Roman Catholic and Protestant positions. Clearly the emphasis on natural law on the part of the Roman Catholic theologians of the past and present has been one reason for the dissimilarity. Another reason is that the more positive relationship between the Christian and the human that one can find in Roman Catholic ethics stands in contrast to many Protestant positions.

Protestant positions *qua* Protestant tend to perceive real discontinuity between the human and the Christian. Roman Catholic ethics has consistently insisted on the goodness of the human and its natural law tradition has consistently claimed that human reason, on the basis of its understanding of humanity, can arrive at a true ethical wisdom and knowledge.

Within the classical Lutheran position the power and efficacy of human reason to discover and establish what is morally right or wrong was incompatible with human sinfulness and the authority of Scripture as the unique source of the knowledge of good and evil.[1]

Within the classical Protestant position the role and value of natural law has been affected by the centrality and primacy given to faith in and revelation of God in Jesus Christ. This is pointedly expressed by Joachim Jeremias. He writes: "One should avoid in the New Testament theology the terms 'Christian morality' and 'Christian ethics' because these expressions are inadequate and liable to misunderstanding. Instead one should speak of 'lived faith.' Then, it is clearly stated that the gift of God precedes His demands."[2]

The classical Protestant position on the role of natural law in ethics is linked to an emphasis on revelation in the Person of Jesus Christ. According to Karl Barth, any attempt to place Christian ethics on the grounding of human reason is to eliminate the paradox of God's revelation in Christ. The revelation of God in Jesus Christ is the sole condition of whatever knowledge we can have of God and of God's will for us. To gain insight into what God's will is and therefore what is morally right and good one needs to turn to Scripture. The ground of ethics itself is in God's word; it does not need grounding from us. Jesus Christ's humanity becomes the norm of our humanity. All anthropological statements must be based exclusively on the revelation of Christ.

Other contemporary Protestant theologians have followed Barth's position. According to W. Shoenfeld, the person of Christ must be the first and the final word when speaking about the foundations of the law.[3] Jacques Ellul moves these positions to their logical end. For Ellul there exists no natural knowledge of justice and the demands of justice only become accessible to humanity through revelation in Christ. "Right and justice are entirely Christocentric."[4]

Emphasis on the role of faith and the revealing function of the person of Jesus Christ appear as characteristics of the Protestant position that distinguish it from the Roman Catholic. Yet the difference between the Catholic and Protestant position is not as clearly defined as it appears.

---

[1] James Gustafson, *Protestant and Roman Catholic Ethics* (Chicago, Univ. of Chicago Press, 1978) p. 14.
[2] Joachim Jeremias, *The Sermon on the Mount* (Phil: Fortress Press, 1963) p. 35.
[3] W. Shoenfeld, *Grundlegung der Rechtswissenschaft* (Stuttgart, 1951) p. 228.
[4] J. Ellul, *Le Fondement Théologique du Droit* (Neuchâtel, 1946) p. 52.

In Catholic thought natural law has been seen as a metaphysical and ahistorical concept referring to the human as such apart from either the Fall or grace. The Protestant position presents a concept of the human that takes into consideration the historical dimension, the actual human condition. That has become an important element for some Roman Catholic theologians and a point of encounter with Protestant positions.

As we have already seen, there has been within the Roman Catholic context a move towards a more Christological understanding of natural law. Natural law, grounded in the act of God the Creator, is, for Fuchs, no less grounded in Christ.[5] Natural law grounded in the creative act of God is also grounded in the re-creative act of God. Thus Christ is the prototype and norm of the human. The Constitution *Gaudium et Spes* gives us a good example of this type of position. This Constitution constantly and pressingly presents Jesus Christ as the "new man" and the true answer to the mystery of human destiny. Christianity proclaims that in Christ the human ideal for which all people strive has been attained in history and, in fact, that unless one is human as Christ was human, one cannot be human at all. Jesus Christ is not only the revelation of God but also the revelation of humanity. In him the questions as to who is God and who is human are answerable only in their complementarity, not as two questions but as one. The Constitution *Gaudium et Spes* affirms this truth in many ways.[6] Jesus Christ is presented as the one who decodes the mystery that human reality is to itself. Humanhood is defined in terms of Jesus Christ. So a "natural law" understanding of morality and a "Christian" understanding of morality cannot be essentially different. There can be no conflict between the ideals of a Christian ethic and the moral ideals to be found in humanity itself.

The Christological emphasis present in the Protestant positions and often considered as a distinctive characteristic of its ethics is also present in some Roman Catholic positions. Yet the Roman Catholic positions on the specificity of Christian ethics remain different. There is another emphasis present in the Protestant positions that has a clear impact on the question of the specificity of Christian ethics, namely the roles of rev-

---

[5] See Josef Fuchs, *Natural Law: A Theological Investigation* (N.Y.: Sheed and Ward, 1965).

[6] Cf. chp. 1 footnote 13, *Pastoral Constitution on the Church in the Modern World*, No. 22, p. 922.

elation and Scripture. In the various Protestant positions we have described, revelation and Scripture as basic sources for morality were understood in different ways. We saw that Gustafson has a weak doctrine of revelation and Scripture. For Karl Barth, revelation and Scripture are *the* reasons for the distinctive character of Christian ethics. Christian ethics is not just a certain type of ethics in general, but rather has its own methodology: all moral knowledge for the making of moral judgments is limited to the revelation which has been given in Jesus Christ, and expressed in the New Testament. Christian moral action is fundamentally an active response to God's Word, Jesus Christ.

As such, Christian ethics is unconditional because it comes from an unconditional source. In Jesus Christ a new humanity is present; and only in Jesus Christ is this new humanity revealed. In the Scriptures we have "revealed morality." The crucial word here is "revealed." In the more fundamentalistic approach, revelation is understood primarily as "divinely given" propositions. Within Protestantism the implications of Scripture as the only source for Christian ethics can be expressed in two questions: "What is the authority of Scripture for ethics? How is Scripture relevant to, or applied to, practical moral matters?"[7]

The same two questions need also to be asked within Roman Catholicism, although the questions have not been as urgent because of the role played by natural law. Vatican II affirmed that the Scriptures are the supreme rule of the Church's faith because, inspired by God and consigned once and for all in writing, they immutably communicate the word of God Himself.[8] Richard McCormick, a theologian who maintains that there is

---

[7] Cf. J. Gustafson, *Protestant and Roman Catholic Ethics*, op. cit., p. 20.

[8] "In His goodness and wisdom, God chose to reveal Himself and to make known to us the hidden purpose of His will (cf. Eph. 1:9) by which through Christ, the Word made flesh, man has access to the Father in the Holy Spirit and comes to share in the divine nature (cf. Eph. 2:18; 2 Pet. 1:4). Through this revelation, therefore, the invisible God (cf. Col. 1:15; 1 Tim. 1:17) out of the abundance of His love speaks to men as friends (cf. Ex. 33:11; Jn. 15:14–15) and lives among them (cf. Bar. 3:38), so that He may invite and take them into fellowship with Himself. This plan of revelation is realized by deeds and words having inner unity: the deeds wrought by God in the history of salvation manifest and confirm the teaching and realities signified by the words, while the words proclaim the deeds and clarify the mystery contained in them. By this revelation then, the deepest truth about God and the salvation of man is made clear to us in Christ, who is the Mediator and at the

no specific Christian ethics, criticized Gustafson's lack of appreciation of revelation and Scripture in morality. "Gustafson's ethics is quite simply not decisively related to Jesus Christ, and he clearly acknowledges this. I cannot accept that, nor do I believe it warranted by biblical materials or the constant reflection on and appropriation of these materials over the centuries by the Christian community."[9] McCormick continues,

> I am forced to conclude that Gustafson views Scripture as a merely human source. I say 'merely' because it is clear that biblical inspiration cannot prescind from human instrumentality. But divine inspiration is not part of Gustafson's analysis or vocabulary. Neither, therefore, is the notion of biblical revelation.
>
> All one can do at this point is to note that this is not the Christian, certainly not the Catholic understanding of Scripture. That understanding is succinctly stated by Vatican II.[10]

For McCormick revelation and Scripture are fundamental realities within the Christian tradition and do play an essential role in the area of ethics.

The reason or reasons for the diversity in positions on the question of the specificity of Christian ethics must be located elsewhere than in the area of natural law, Christology, or revelation. The one emphasis that is consistently present in the various Protestant positions is that of the role of the Church. In Roman Catholic morality the revelation which the Church has the responsibility of communicating is the revelation of the possibility of the fulfillment of the potential of natural man/woman. What is emphasized about the Church is its magisterial function, a function without which natural morality would remain in ignorance of how it is called upon to realize itself. In Protestantism morality can be defined in terms of right relationships, with God, with the neighbor, with oneself. As such it is a morality animated from within by faith, a faith nurtured and developed within an ecclesial community. In the Protestant positions we have a reassertion of the significance of the Church in the area of ethics. This is the one characteristic that is consistently part of

---

same time the fullness of all revelation." From *Dei Verbum*, in *The Documents of Vatican II*, ed. Walter M. Abbott (New York: America Press, 1966), p. 112.

[9]Richard A. McCormick, "Gustafson's God: Who? What? Where? (Etc.)," *The Journal of Religious Ethics*, Vol. 131, Spring (1985) p. 67.

[10]Ibid., pp. 66–67.

the contemporary Protestant theological tradition, conservative or liberal. Schleiermacher had already rejected the value of natural theology on the insight that the truth of the Christian religion cannot be discerned apart from the historical world and the experiencing of it. And the concrete form which this world takes for the Christians is the Church. Far from being led to a mere "ecclesiology," there emerged a realization that the reality of the Church becomes the focal point of orientation for a theology of the history of faith and revelation and the central theme for a discussion of the specificity of Christian ethics.

Dialectical Theology and the Role of the Church in Ethics

For dialectical theology the Church must deal with the question of how revelation can enter into relationship with human reality without losing its proper distinctiveness. But the distinction between the word of revelation and everything else in the world and its immunity from human control must remain unimpaired in the process. The Church is the locus of revelation; the reality of the Church is the definition of revelation in terms of its consequences. Thus the Church serves the hermeneutic of revelation; this is so for Barth and Bultmann. The Church defines the otherness of God in the act of revelation and maintains it unimpaired in the communicating of the Word. For Barth revelation creates a history of its own which remains transcendent over all other history and its continuities and which is defined by the Church.[11]

During the attempt at the Nazification of the churches in Germany, the confessing Church resisted. It did so by affirming that "Jesus, as he is witnessed to in Holy Scripture, is the one Word of God to whom we must listen, whom we must trust and obey in life and in death."[12] That obedience to God's Word engages its listeners to loyalty; it is made public in the Church: and known, not within the solitary life of individuals but in the common life of the Church. So for Karl Barth, while God addresses individual persons God does so inasmuch as they are part of a

---

[11] See Trutz Rendtorff, *Church and Theology. The Systematic Function of the Church Concept in Modern Theology* (Phil.: Westminster Press, 1971).

[12] Robin W. Lovin, *Christian Faith and Public Choices* (Phil: Fortress Press, 1984) p. 102.

people. The faith of the individual must be located within the faith of the Church. It is in the proclaimed or preached Word of God and therefore within the Church that God's Word is heard.

> The language about God to be found in the Church is meant to be proclamation, so far as it is directed towards man in the form of preaching and sacrament, with the claim and in an atmosphere of expectation that in accordance with its commission it has to tell him the Word of God to be heard in faith.[13]
>
> The Word of God is God Himself in the proclamation of the Church of Jesus Christ. In so far as God gives the Church the commission to speak about Him, and the Church discharges this commission, it is God Himself who declares His revelation in His witnesses. The proclamation of the Church is pure doctrine when the human word spoken in it in confirmation of the biblical witness to revelation offers and creates obedience to the Word of God.[14]

What is being affirmed by Barth is the "revelatory character of the Church" and the ecclesial nature of theology and ethics.

The importance of the Church in ethics is also emphasized by Hauerwas and Gustafson. Stanley Hauerwas has written that the authority of Scripture in the area of ethics cannot be separated from an existing believing community. He writes: "The meaning of authority must be grounded in a community's self-understanding, which is embodied in its habits, customs, laws, and traditions; for this embodiment constitutes the community's pledge to provide the means for an individual more nearly to approach the truth."[15] Authority grounded in community is what tradition is all about. To attribute authority to Scripture in the area of ethics means for Christians " . . . that they find there the traditions through which their community most nearly comes to knowing and being faithful to the truth. Scripture is not meant to be a problem-solver, it rather describes the process whereby the community we call the Church is initiated by certain texts into what Barth has called the 'vivid and lively

---

[13] Karl Barth, "The Doctrine of the Word of God," *Church Dogmatics* I/1 (Edinburgh: T. and T. Clark, 1936) p. 5.

[14] K. Barth, *Church Dogmatics*, I/2, op. cit., pp. 7–13.

[15] S. Hauerwas, *A Community of Character*, p. 60.

pattern of argument and controversy' characteristic of biblical traditions."[16]

Gustafson has made the same point in his attempt to establish a theocentric ethic. He has stressed the essential role of communities of moral discourse.[17] He writes:

> The purpose of moral discourse in communities is not in most cases to come to a unanimous conclusion, though there are occasions when this is proper. It is to help form the "consciences" of persons, to educate their rational activity, to enable them to think more clearly and thoroughly about the moral dimensions of aspects of life in the world. It is to hone more sharply their moral thinking from which choices and actions in part flow.[18]

Emphasis on the role of the Church in the area of ethics does not imply that all theologians hold the same doctrine of Church. For Barth, the Church is the locus of Revelation; for Gustafson it is simply a natural society. Yet for both theologians the Church plays an important role in the area of ethics.

This emphasis on the role of the Church is not unrelated to Christology. Earlier on in this century it was often affirmed that every formulation of an ecclesiology depended upon and implied a christological foundation. To know a theologian's Christology was to know a great deal about his/her ecclesiology.[19] While this affirmation is true to a large extent, there is also another dimension to the situation; Christology is clearly the product of the Church. The quest for the historical Jesus, an attempt to bypass the Church's interpretation, failed; in its attempt it reinforced the role of the earlier Church in the formulation of a Chris-

---

[16] Ibid., p. 63.

[17] See James M. Gustafson, "The Church: A Community of Moral Discourse," in *The Church as Moral Decision Maker* (Philadelphia: Pilgrim Press, 1970) pp. 83–95; also "The University as a Community of Moral Discourse," *The Journal of Religion* 53 (1973), pp. 397–409.

[18] James Gustafson, *Ethics From a Theocentric Perspective*, Vol. 2 Ethics and Theology (Chicago: Univ. of Chicago Press, 1984) p. 317.

[19] This is well recognized by both Yves Congar and T. W. Manson. The latter roundly says that "the doctrine of the Church is a branch of Christology": Thomas W. Manson, *The Church's Ministry* (London: Hodder and Stoughton, 1948) p. 20.

tology. Redaction criticism has emphasized that much of the material in the Gospels must be ascribed to the theological motivation of the evangelist within a specific context. This means that in practice we must take as our starting point the assumption that the Gospels offer us directly information about the theology of the early Church and not about the teaching of the historical Jesus.

Christology is a product of the Church; but one can go further and affirm that Christology is ecclesiology. It is in the unpacking of this affirmation that it will become apparent why the Church does not play an important role in ethics from the perspective of the Roman Catholic positions. At the beginning of this century Adolph von Harnack attempted to answer the question: What is the essence of Christianity? His answer: Jesus' preaching of the Kingdom of God; God's rule within the hearts of individuals, a rule that demands a conversion. That Kingdom is not the Church; the Church is a necessary but deficient embodiment of Jesus' Gospel.[20] Yet, as F. Schussler-Fiorenza writes: "For Harnack the Gospel has need of a Church because the believer cannot discover within herself or himself the means of salvation."[21]

In his attempt to refute Harnack's chasm between the historical Jesus and the Church, Alfred Loisy in his *The Gospel and the Church* [22] initiated a controversy within the Roman Catholic Church with consequences in contemporary thought. While affirming that there is a fundamental continuity between Jesus' proclamation of the Kingdom and the emergence of the Church, he also wrote: "It is certain, for instance, that Jesus did not systematize beforehand the constitution of the Church as that of a government established on earth and destined to endure for a long series of centuries."[23] With this affirmation, as F. Schüssler Fiorenza writes, "The historical question about the relation between the Church and the earthly Jesus came to the forefront as a modern controversy within theology and especially within Roman Catholic theol-

---

[20] Adolph von Harnack, *What is Christianity?*, tr. T. B. Saunders (New York: Harper, 1957).

[21] F. Schüssler-Fiorenza, *Foundational Theology* (New York: Crossroad Publishing, 1984), p. 63.

[22] Alfred Loisy, *The Gospel and the Church,* trans. Christopher Home (Philadelphia: Fortress, 1976).

[23] Ibid., p. 166.

ogy."[24] The basic question in ecclesiology became that of its foundation. While that question can lead to a purely apologetical ecclesiology, it does however concern also "the large systematic issue of the meaning of Jesus and of Christianity. In what does the Christian vision consist? What is the reality of Christianity? How does the historical development of ecclesial Christianity relate to Jesus and to the vision present in his preaching and in his life-praxis?"[25]

As it became clear that historically one could not demonstrate that Jesus instituted the Church, existential and transcendental approaches to the nature of the Church emerged. Such approaches are present in Karl Rahner's theology. For Rahner, Christianity affirms that in Jesus, God has given this world an absolute savior, an irreversible historical offer of salvation and an offer which by necessity implies and demands an on-going faith in Jesus Christ. Yet for Rahner, before an individual has heard the good news of Christianity, his/her subjectivity is already graced, and prepared to hear the explicit preaching of the Gospel and recognize it as fulfilling her/his own potentialities. All the religions including the Christian tradition are explicitations of humanity's graced subjectivity. Yet humanity's attempt to express and reflect upon its transcendence contains a mixture of truth and error. Thus there is a need for a criterion or evaluation. What is the graced element in the religions; how are we to know which are true or false?

Here Rahner emphasizes the role of the prophet. Prophets are those "persons in whom the self-interpretation of this supernatural, transcendental experience and its history takes place in word and deed."[26] Rahner goes even further and affirms that "the prophet is none other than the believer who can express his transcendental experience of God correctly."[27] All human history is the history of grace yet it is a history that is ambivalent; made of truth and error. And while profane history and salvation history are co-extensive they are also distinct; God undertakes to interpret part of this profane and ambiguous history through the Word. While this interpretation occurs in the history of Israel and is recorded in the Old Testament, it becomes clearly and finally interpreted in Jesus

---

[24] F. Schüssler-Fiorenza, *Foundational Theology*, op. cit., pp. 63–64.
[25] Ibid., p. 24.
[26] Karl Rahner, *Foundations of Christian Faith*, op. cit., p. 158.
[27] Ibid., p. 159.

Christ, who is the final and unsurpassable "criterion for distinguishing in the concrete history of religion what is a human misunderstanding of the transcendental experience of God, and what is the legitimate interpretation of this experience."[28] Historical Christianity is the concrete, objective, and thematized enunciation of humanity's graced transcendence. "It is to be expected that this divinized ground of man will everywhere and always . . . try to become the object of reflection, driven to this by the very dynamism of grace under a supernatural, saving providence of God. It is to be expected that it will try to objectify itself in explicit expressions of religion, such as in the liturgy and religious associations and in protests of a 'prophetic' kind . . ."[29]

Rahner shows that the Incarnation is unique and gratuitous, the fulfillment of the evolutionary process. "The incarnation of the Logos . . . appears as the ontologically . . . unambiguous goal of the movement of creation as a whole, in relation to which everything prior is merely a preparation of the scene. . . ."[30] The Incarnation appears oriented from the very proximity to and distance from what is other than the Incarnate. The Incarnation is the fulfillment of the evolutionary process of creation, for in Jesus Christ evolution has reached its climax and goal. The Incarnation is an intrinsic moment within the evolutionary process already graced and temporally if not ontologically preceding the Incarnation. It is within this evolutionary process that Jesus Christ appears as the absolute savior. For faith in the absolute savior, if it is to endure, must be communal and public and therefore be historically tangible. The need and nature of faith in Jesus as absolute savior demands the existence of a Church. The existence of a Church is necessitated also by the fact that human existence is essentially interpersonal, and the Christian religion therefore must be ecclesial.[31]

While this position appears quite similar to that of Loisy, it is profoundly different. Not only is the Church necessary to bring the preached Jesus to each generation, it is the necessary symbolization of God's

---

[28] Ibid., p. 157.

[29] Karl Rahner, "History of the World and Salvation History," *Theological Investigations* V (London: Darton, Longman and Todd, 1966) p. 105.

[30] Karl Rahner, "Current Problems in Christology," *Theological Investigations* I (London: Darton, Longman and Todd, 1961) p. 165.

[31] K. Rahner, *Foundations of Christian Faith*, op. cit., pp. 322–23.

grace. Indeed the Church and Jesus have the same function. Since salvation is offered to all, the Church can include all of humanity; it can also be a specific institution. There is an inner connection not only between faith in Christ and the ecclesial expression of that faith, but also between ecclesial existence and human existence. The Church is truly the sacrament of Christ as Christ is the sacrament of God. As such the Church has the same sacramental function as Jesus Christ; it symbolizes the grace of God in the world.

We have seen that Rahner's transcendental approach influenced most of the contemporary approaches to the question of specificity of Christian ethics. It established the foundations for the distinction between transcendental morality and categorical morality, the specificity of Christian ethics being situated on the transcendental level much more than on the categorical level. At the transcendental level the specificity of Christian ethics escapes the influence of the Church in the same way that the Church escapes the narrowing effects of history. What is known in and through Christ, and therefore in and through the Church, in the sphere of the moral cannot be inconsistent with what is known through our humanness. Christian morality is a human morality in the best sense of the word and the moral conduct of the Christian must essentially be human conduct. Christ as sacrament of God and the Church as sacrament of Christ are prototypes and norms of the human; as such they are not historical norms to be distinguished essentially from the norms of common humanness. Christ and the Church make explicitly Christian what can be implicit in the consciousness of all women and men. The difference in the specific area of ethics is between explicit and implicit, not between more or less. The mediation of Christ, of the Church or of our humanness is basically and ultimately the same, differing only as explicit to implicit.

Christhood is seen as the fulfillment of humanity, the expression of what authentic humanity needs to be. The key concept in this approach is "transcendent anthropology." A "transcendent anthropology" is one that emphasizes the transcendental character of human subjectivity. Such a subjectivity is characterized by a universally experienced directedness toward God. A gracious "supernatural existential" is constitutive of what is normatively human. This gracious existential is always mediated historically. This mediation is named "categorical."

Human reality in both its transcendental and its categorical dimensions is oriented towards an "absolute savior." Hence Rahner can write:

> Christian anthropology is only able to fulfill its whole purpose if it understands man as the potentia oboedientialis for the "Hypostatic Union." And Christology can only be undertaken from the point of view of this kind of transcendental anthropology; for in order to say today what the "Hypostatic Union" is without being suspected of merely reproducing no longer feasible "mythologies," the idea of the God-man needs proof of a transcendental orientation in man's being and history under grace.[32]

The transcendental approach to anthropology as applied to Christology and ecclesiology emphasizes a basic distinction between the transcendental and categorical. We have seen that this distinction plays an important role in the Roman Catholic position on the specificity of Christian ethics. At the categorical level where virtues and norms are realized, Christian ethics has no real specificity; it is the transcendental dimension that distinguishes Christian morality. This transcendentality or intentionality is oriented in a special way toward God in Christ. Christian morality is not unique, but it bears a different transcendental intentionality. Yet at both levels there is only one basic imperative "Be human," that is, the transcendental intentionality makes explicit what is already present in the concreteness of human existence.

Rahner's position has been criticized from different sources. A common criticism has been directed to the transcendental method. J. B. Metz accused Rahner of being too dependent on German idealism and therefore of underestimating the importance of the concreteness of historical and social subjects. The method promotes an idealized universality constituted in a preapprehension of God. A transcendental deduction of the Church tends to undermine the basic historical/social structure of the Church. In the area of ethics, the Christological approach to natural law appears as individualistic; as an attempt to ground moral norms in an "a priori realm to secure for moral judgment an objectivity that would free such judgments from the subjective beliefs, wants and

---

[32] K. Rahner, "Theology and Anthropology," *Theological Investigations* IX (N.Y.: Herder and Herder, 1972) 28–29.

stories of the agent who makes them."[33] Moral consciousness is shaped in the concreteness of everyday life, not in a transcendental notion of "value" which would ground all our questions about value. The point of departure for Christian ethics cannot be a transcendental experience, nor a transcendental openness to the acceptance of Revelation in Jesus Christ but rather must be an experience that takes place within a concrete cultural situation in relation to a concrete religious history. A transcendental approach is always in danger of minimizing the historical concreteness of this experience. The openness of the transcendental subjectivity is a point of arrival and not a point of departure. The starting point of a Christian ethics must be the concrete beliefs, symbols, and hopes of Christianity, the disclosive power of the New Testament and not a transcendental analysis of human nature.

The Roman Catholic theologians affirm that the specificity of Christian ethics lies in the area of faith or intentionality. While materially there is only one morality common to Christians and non-Christians, formally there is a distinction, for faith creates a distinctiveness in our intentionality. Prescinding from this intentionality Christian morality is in its materiality and concreteness purely a human morality. Yet such an intentionality cannot be purely formal. It simply cannot be too easily affirmed as belonging to the realm of the transcendental and not the categorical. The Christian intentionality envisioned as the primary element of the specificity of Christian ethics is directly related to the particular, to the categorical. Intentionality is never abstract but always contextual and historically conditioned. Intentionality takes place within a cultural tradition that provides concepts and paradigms according to which that intentionality is interpreted. There can be no radical distinction made between the concreteness of moral existence and the intentionality that lies behind such a reality. At the level of intentionality and materiality there is no religious ethical decision that can escape the influence of the historical tradition.

While Protestantism was accused by Catholicism of being thoroughly individualistic because of the way Scripture was interpreted, this is clearly not the case relative to the process of becoming an ethical per-

---

[33]John Yoder, *The Politics of Jesus* (Grand Rapids: W. Eerdmans, 1972), p. 141. See also John H. Yoder, "The Hermeneutics of Peoplehood: A Protestant Perspective on Practical and Moral Reasoning," *Journal of Religious Ethics* 10 (1982) pp. 40–67.

son. What was excluded by Protestantism was the role of the hierarchy as interpreter of Scripture, not the role of the Church. While the role of the hierarchy is emphasized in Catholicism, that of the communal and formative nature of the ecclesial community is not. Thus despite the long stress on the role of the Church's hierarchy to decide what is right or wrong in the area of morality, the importance of the communities of faith was not stressed. A transcendental approach to the Church does not help overcome this deficiency. It does not lead to the recognition of the particular character of each moral agent and the role of the communities of faith in identifying and shaping the moral perceptions of their members.

Differences on the questions of the nature and purpose of the Church have important consequences for Christian ethics. While Protestant churches do not claim infallible authority in matters of morality, they do claim a function as moral teachers. The Church is not there to dictate moral conduct, but to constantly propose and promote the Gospel. In Protestantism morality depends on an ongoing formative educational process. The Christian community is understood as the matrix of the Christian conscience, rather than as a prescriber of moral propositions. The concept of the Church is one of the clues to the understanding of the nature of Christian ethics. The universality of human reality and the distinctiveness of Christianity are not made directly dependent on one another but through the mediation of the Church are indirectly related to one another.

IV.

Specific Christian Ethics and the Role of Tradition

Our survey of Roman Catholic and Protestant positions on the question of the specificity of Christian ethics has indicated a fundamental diversity on the function and formative role of the ecclesial communities in the realm of ethics. While most Protestant positions emphasize the formative role of ecclesial communities, Roman Catholic ethicists, on the other hand, seem to pay little attention to the formative role of the religious traditions out of which they write. Emphasis is given to the authority of the magisterium in the interpretation of ethical norms, but not to the formative role of the ecclesial community as such. Now this perspective, i.e. the role of the ecclesial community in ethics, must certainly have repercussions not only on the acceptance or refusal of the existence of a specific Christian ethics, but also on the nature and process of such an ethic, for the emphasis on the formative role of ecclesial communities in the realm of ethics implies a renewed emphasis on tradition, on the role of history of narratives and imagination and therefore on hermeneutics as a fundamental task for Christian ethics.

Emphasis on the formative role of ecclesial communities in ethics implies emphasis on the role and function of tradition. Contemporary thought in both the secular and the religious realms has emphasized the importance of tradition in the structuring of communal and personal identities. It is not accidental that one of the major theological achievements of the Second Vatican Council was its teaching on tradition. Vatican II proposed a total notion of "Tradition":

> The Church, in her doctrine, life, and worship, perpetuates and transmits . . . all that she herself is, all that she believes . . . its riches are poured out in the practice and life of the Church, in her belief and prayer; . . . the holy Scriptures themselves are more thoroughly understood and constantly actualized in the Church; . . . the Spirit, through whom the living Gospel rings out in the Church—and through her in the world—leads believers to the full truth and makes the Word of Christ dwell in them in all its richness.[1]

Tradition is not understood as the mere transmission of doctrine but as the total reality of the Church. Tradition is identified with the being and faith of the Church. This is a dynamic understanding of tradition. It emphasizes the traditionary process.

Tradition's contribution to the development of the human community is threefold: it is a source for communal and personal identity; it provides a system of communication which is a source of unity; and it makes possible continuity plus the integration of change and creativity. Tradition provides resources for personal and communal identities. It does so in positive and negative ways. It provides boundaries which, by dividing the world into "us" and "not us," provide a form of identification. Boundaries appear basically in roles, in hierarchy markers, and in scales of valuation. Such elements become the basic source of our identity and the formation of our ego and ethical selves.

World views, symbols, and rationales for group boundaries are expressed in narratives, myths and rituals. As a container for such material, tradition is a communication system providing cohesion and continuity. According to Robert Schreiter, tradition "provides a semiotic system, a set of codes within that system whereby the basic messages of identity can circulate through a culture."[2] Since personal identity is not simply a given but an accomplishment, tradition provides a matrix that guarantees cohesion and continuity. As such, tradition also provides a process for the incorporation of change and creativity and even dissonance.

Since tradition plays such an important role, it is necessary to speak

---

[1] *Dei Verbum*, Ch II, No 8, pp. 115–116.
[2] Robert Schreiter, *Constructing Local Theologies* (Maryknoll: Orbis Books, 1985), p. 106.

about the fundamentally social character of selfhood. Personal identity is the result of a process of socialization. Socialization involves the process of being inserted into a social-cultural environment which in fact produces one's self-identity. That process of insertion demands the internalization of the society's self-understanding, self-image, and valuing. Thomas Groome, paraphrasing Herbert Mead, writes:

> Having externalized ourselves into culture and society, and culture and society having taken on a life of their own, the empowerments and limitations of that world are now taken back into our consciousness as our own. The possibilities and parameters that our social/cultural context appears to offer become our own perception of our possibilities and parameters. In other words, the objectified culture and society created by us and our predecessors become internalized as the basis of our own self-identity.[3]

Human persons are not socialized simply by being instructed into a tradition; they are also constituted by the tradition. The temporality and historicity of the individual is specified by the tradition.

The social character of human selfhood does not in itself undercut individual and group identity and liberty but forms the context in which these can be more fully realized.

The process of socialization determines the process of self-interpretation. As Joseph Cahill says: "... in many instances this self-interpretation is really a misnomer since the interpretation is really done by others rather than by a genuinely autonomous or inner-directed self."[4] In this context a new self-interpretation, a new self-image is never simple or easy. One of the basic problems inherent in the process of socialization is the fact that social structures and cultural patterns tend to be conservative and to overwhelm the individual.

The corporate belief of a community seems to provide the necessary matrix for the emergence of personal creeds, that appear to the individual as "something totally different." While the possibilities and parameters

---

[3] Thomas Groome, *Christian Religious Education* (San Francisco: Harper and Row, 1980), p. 112.
[4] Joseph Cahill, *Mended Speech: The Crisis of Religious Studies and Theology* (N.Y.: Crossroad, 1982), p. 154.

intrinsic to tradition tend to become the individual's own, yet the individual is not ultimately determined by the socialization process. Change can occur; the individual can be critical and needs to be critical of his/her cultural-social structures. While the individual appropriates his/her identity through the internalization of the community's self-understanding, yet he/she is not fully determined by the ecclesial reality. The interaction between the self and the community is dialectical and involves necessarily some tensions which can be creative yet always conflictual.

As J. Cahill writes:

> In the active sense tradition gives identity to the individual while at the same time gradually involving one in one's own hermeneutic, one's own choice as to how one will understand oneself within the tradition that initially gave identity. It is the tradition which enables the individual to remember a past and look forward to a future. In both the active and passive senses, there is a noetic structure to tradition. This noetic structure makes the tradition and subsequently, but to a lesser degree, the individual comprehensible. Because of the dynamism of human existence and because of the cultural evolution following this dynamism, tradition is susceptible to change, growth, decline, modification, and sometimes to obscurity or the ambiguous state I will later describe as dissonance. But by definition all mutation is gradual—even in so-called revolutionary societies. There is then a communality in structure and function among all traditions.[5]

It is through a traditionary process that one arrives at a Christian identity. In Romans 10:13–15, Paul outlines the basic process that governs access to Christian existence: "Everyone who invokes the name of the Lord will be saved." How could they invoke one in whom they had no faith? And how could they have faith in one they had never heard of? And how hear without someone to spread the news? And how could anyone spread the news without a commission to do so? And that is what Scripture affirms: "How welcome are the feet of the messengers of good news!" Faith in Christ, and therefore Christian existence, is essentially ecclesial. The Church is the prime recipient of the Gospel. Only in connection with the Church does the individual have access to the reve-

---

[5]Ibid., pp. 58–59.

lation of God in Jesus Christ. Faith in Christ is inseparable from the Church. The Church is essentially a mediating reality, spatial and historical. Accepting Ernest Troeltsch's important insight, David Tracy writes, "It is the tradition of the church that is our central mediation to the actual Jesus—the Jesus remembered by the church; it is our present experience of that mediated Christ-event which impels our belief in Jesus Christ . . ."[6]

The present experience of the Christ-event is mediated through the tradition. Trust in the reality of the Christ-event as made present to us implies essentially trust in the mediation itself.[7] The tradition is an essential structure in the emergence of Christian existence and identity. Tracy writes, "We live in the Christ-event in and by the tradition, the community, the church."[8]

The Christ-event is mediated through the particular historical form that the Christian Church is. Thus, the Church as tradition is the way for the organization of human experience as Christian. This systematic organization is a communal possession which provides stability and an effective way of living for the believer. As Christians, individuals are socialized and constituted by the Christian tradition. It is the Christian tradition which enables the individual to remember the past Christ-event, celebrate its actual presence and anticipate its future fulfillment. The tradition plays an integrating role by uniting past, present, and future. The Christian community formed by the Christian tradition is a community of memory, celebration, and expectation.

The Church's own theological affirmations arose out of its responses to the Christ-event as related in the Scriptures; these responses shaped the self-understanding of its members. The process of socialization not only carries a tradition from the past into the present but also provides for the internalization of its meanings by those who participate in it. Gustafson expresses clearly this process:

> In many respects one becomes a Christian in the same way that one becomes identifiable by any other social distinction—nationality, class and so on. The stories, symbols, cultic life, preaching, and other

---

[6] David Tracy, *The Analogical Imagination* (N.Y.: Crossroad, 1981), p. 323.
[7] Ibid.
[8] Ibid.

aspects of institutional religious life provide the participant with a perspective from which to respond affectively and intentionally to nature, historical events, culture, society, and themselves. Persons may drift away from these symbols and their meanings as those of other communities provide a more satisfying way to form the persons' aspirations, interpret the events in which they participate, and judge their own worthiness. Persons may consciously reject them in the light of what they perceive to be illusions, repressiveness, intellectual weakness, or defective morality. Or they may rigidly and dogmatically hold certain symbols and meanings to be orthodox, adhere to them as the exclusive ways to interpret the meanings of events and experiences, and close themselves off from anything that would threaten the security that the tradition offers. But the tradition, expressed in various forms, does inform those who participate in it.[9]

The current interest in narrative for the establishing of religious and moral identity is simply the result of our understanding of the process of socialization. The introduction of narrative into the discussion of moral theology encourages reflective inquiry into those activities of the Christian community which present to it the sharing images of Christian life and which form Christian moral existence. Discussion of community and narrative help to make clear that an individual's moral life is anchored in the life and history of a community in virtue of shared vision, moral sensitivities, attitudes and imagination.

The importance of narrative leads to a re-appreciation of memory and imagination in the emergence of Christian identity. Growing out of a religion in which remembering played such a critical role, it is not at all surprising that memory and imagination would also be important. According to Herbert Musurillo, "there is, or at least should be, a specifically Christian imagination, one that has been elevated by Baptism into the mystical Body, and has been impregnated by the truths, symbols and liturgy of revelation."[10] Karl Rahner emphasizes the same point:

> Has not our phantasy (imagination) too been consecrated down to the deepest roots of man since the eternal Word became flesh? And

---

[9]James M Gustafson, *Ethics From a Theocentric Perspective*, Vol. II: Ethics and Theology (Chicago: University of Chicago Press, 1984), p. 231.

[10]Herbert Musurillo, *Symbolism and the Christian Imagination* (Baltimore: Helicon Press, 1962), p. 3.

> should the image which faith creates out of this fact and in which it is concentrated and embodied, not be a kind of quasisacramental sign which sanctifies and blesses, guards and enlightens? I naturally include under the heading of "image" everything which belongs to the realm of sensibility, and not only what is ordered to the sense of sight and therefore words, sounds, signs, gestures, in short everything in which the celestial spirit can be embodied, the nether depths of our being sanctified and the spirit of earth banished.[11]

For Kathleen Fischer, our encounter with God is fundamentally linked to our imagination.

> It is on the level of the imagination that we first encounter the divine in this world, for revelation is always given through the material: it is always symbolic, pointing to the ultimate through the finite. It is also on the level of the imagination that we formulate our initial response to the encounter with the divine; faith finds expression first as myth and ritual, sacrament, symbol, image and story. Only later does it become dogma and institution.[12]

The importance of memory and imagination in our journey to God has implications for our understanding of revelation and faith. Avery Dulles has emphasized the role of symbol and therefore of imagination in revelation. According to Dulles, revelation "is mediated through symbol—that is to say, through an externally perceived sign that works mysteriously on the human consciousness so as to suggest more than it can clearly describe or define."[13]

Revelation reaches us through symbols, which presupposes that "God's self-communication is always mediated to us through the experience of the world. How else can revelation reach us, since we our-

---

[11] Karl Rahner, "A Spiritual Dialogue at Evening: On Sleep, Prayer, and Other Subjects," in *Theological Investigations*, Vol. III. *The Theology of the Spiritual Life* trans. Karl H and Boniface Kruger (London: Darton, Longman and Todd,1967), p. 233.

[12] Kathleen R. Fischer, *The Inner Rainbow: The Imagination in Christian Life* (New York: Paulist Press), 1983. p. 3.

[13] Avery Dulles, S.J., "The Symbolic Structure of Revelation," *Theological Studies*, Vol 41, No. 1 (March 1980), pp. 55–56.

selves are incarnate spirits who know the invisible only through its visible and material forms?"[14]

In the life of faith, then, images are more fundamental than ideas or concepts insofar as they precede ideas and concepts. Fischer notes that "we do not believe **in** the images themselves, we see **through** them. If we do not see through them, they can get in the way and restrict our vision. An image or metaphor is like a lens through which we catch a glimpse of God."[15]

In Christianity, the Incarnation is the most complete statement of the divine disclosure in symbolic form. Christ himself is the fundamental symbol and image for Christians, and it is in the sacramental life of the Church that the symbolic dimension of the Christ-event is predominant. The symbolic and narrative nature of the liturgy again emphasizes the role of imagination. As social ecclesial rituals, the liturgy and the sacraments call to mind beliefs, intensify values, and express the Christian tradition for the faithful. The liturgical and sacramental life of the church is then a central component of the Christian formation process.

Liturgy and sacraments help us to underscore the communal nature of the tradition. Christian faith and formation are not individual matters, but depend upon a community of believers. They underscore the importance and power of memory and imagination in the formation of Christian identity and commitment.

If tradition is so essential to the formation of one's identity and the Christian tradition for one's Christian identity, the very nature of ethics and of Christian ethics cannot be unrelated to tradition. There can be no such thing as reliance on pure simple reason or pure simple faith.

All our morality is social—we are inherently social—and, as Durkheim and many others have clearly indicated, what makes us so uniquely human is the degree to which we are social beings. Our ability for relationship is our most distinctive characteristic. True morality is never a concern with how to live our lives in isolation. It is a concern to participate most fully in human relationship. As essentially social, there is no

---

[14] Ibid., pp. 30–31.
[15] K. Fischer, *The Inner Rainbow*, p. 12.

abstract morality. Christian ethics is anchored in history and cannot escape history; it cannot be freed from historic communities and tradition.

This social nature of Christian ethics is supported by the nature and implications of using the root metaphor of Kingdom of God to express the ideal and reality of Christianity. The Christian concept of the Kingdom of God, with its roots deep in the Old Testament understanding, offers a viable way of understanding the nature and process of Christian ethics. In the Old Testament use of the concept, the Kingdom of God is God's fundamental way of relating to humanity, not through a relationship with individuals, but through a relationship with a people. Even God's relationship to individuals is done as a way of communicating God's will to the people. It is with the social life of the people that God is concerned. Even salvation is understood as primarily a social rather than an individual event. The salvation of the individual demands the salvation of the society. This concept is central to the New Testament understanding of the Kingdom. Individual and social salvation are not separable.

Christian ethics will be based upon the guidance drawn from community and context. Its guidance is concrete, particular, and dependent upon what is available in its present life. Morality will have an essentially communal dimension and cannot simply be a question of individual matter. Now the communal mode of existence is one of communication, of inter-action—one that is shaped by a past history, by a living tradition. The communal mode of existence is essentially contextual; contexts vary and are manifold.[16]

---

[16]Commenting on the meaning of the ethical task, Gordon Kaufman writes the following:

"Man's proper role in life is here assigned him by God; human life finds its true meaning so far as it is a fulfillment of the purposes of God. But since [in the Bible] God is conceived as living and personal—and not as the impersonal structure of nature, as in naturalism—it is not possible to define laws of conduct or right action (corresponding to laws of nature) which hold once and for all. Rather, right action here will simply be living-as-a-person-in-community with God, on the one hand, and one's fellow men, on the other. To live in community, it should be evident, involves much more than merely following out some pattern of absolute values or ideals or laws which have once for all been laid down as norms of conduct. To live in the community is to live in **responsiveness** to other persons in the community, to listen when they speak and to answer honestly and relevantly and significantly, to minister to their needs and to allow them to minister to yours. In short, it is to

Socialization has to do not only with the cognitive dimension of the interactional self but also with its affective dimension—the individual not only internalizes values and perspectives, he/she also takes into him/herself certain deep affective attitudes that color all his/her more specific perspectives. Thus, socialization is not only a cognitive process, it is also an affective process involving the acquisition of deep underlying feelings about oneself and others.

Moral values derive from historical experience within the community of faith. So far as Christianity is concerned, religious ethics has to do with beliefs, values, and actions of persons whose perceptions have somehow been shaped by religious tradition. The religious believer who has been shaped by his/her relation to a believing community is not identical with some abstract natural man/woman; nor is he/she identical with persons shaped by religious communities other than his/her own. The Christian as a moral agent is no abstraction. He/she has been shaped historically, affectively, and socially in and through a tradition. The inherited Christian tradition forms the Christian individual's identity.

All moral agents are particular and individual agents. As such these agents, as moral agents, derive "their uniqueness from the context in which they view themselves and from the history of their own choices."[17] The communities to which one belongs, the media through which one is in contact with the ultimate source of human existence are therefore of real importance in the realm of human ethics and of Christian ethics. Christian faith which demands a conversion which affects human existence at various levels will necessarily affect the moral life. The first question is not "What is God commanding?" but rather "What is God

---

be a living and responsive **thou** to their **I's.**

From this point of view the task of ethics is not the isolating of some ultimate standard of right and wrong, then insisting on conformity to that standard. Rather, the concern here is to be responsive to the voice of the living God as he confronts and speaks to us in every moment, to live as human persons before this supreme Person, that is, to act creatively and freely in every moment in response to his will for that moment. In short, it is to enter into community with God and his other creatures, or to use the biblical symbol, it is to participate in the kingdom of God."

Gordon D. Kaufman, *The Context of Decision: A Theological Analysis* (New York: Abingdon, 1961), pp. 25f.

[17]W.C. Spohn, "The Reasoning Heart: An American Approach to Christian Discernment" in *Theological Studies*, Vol. 44, No. 1 (1983), p. 36.

enabling and requiring me (or us) to be and to do?"[18] In the existential realm, three important aspects of morality are affected and qualified by the Christian experience and beliefs: "the reason for being moral, the character of the moral agent and the points of reference used to determine conduct."[19] From all of these points one can speak of ethics as Christian. For within a specific way of life certain values and principles can have an obligatory character. These values and principles can have universal value not in the abstract, but only through the confirmation of lived experience.

As Spohn writes: "Particular persons derive their uniqueness from the contexts in which they view themselves and from the history of their own choices."[20] Here the self is not understood substantially but interactionally. As Niebuhr writes, "The self is a being which comes to knowledge of itself in the presence of other selves—its very nature is that of a being which lives in response to other selves."[21] Spohn continues:

> The self does not have its meaning because it is an instance of human nature; the meaning of this particular self emerges through dialogue with others. Therefore a new 'root metaphor' is necessary for moral philosophy: the self-as-responder is more adequate to the interactional development of the self than previous root metaphors. These have been self-as-maker, which likens the moral life to a constructive quest for human happiness, and self-as-citizen, which portrays the moral life as a life of obedience to universal laws.[22]

In relation to the question of the distinctiveness of Christian ethics, one must deal with the historical level; one must take into consideration the history of the moral agent, the symbolic resources of imagination and the symbolic complex of the Christian tradition. There is no escape from historicity and particularity. The moral agent must be dealt with as historically conditioned and shaped.

---

[18] J. Gustafson, *Can Ethics Be Christian?* op. cit., pp. 156–57.
[19] Ibid.
[20] W.C. Spohn, *"The Reasoning Heart,"* p. 36.
[21] H. Richard Niebuhr, *The Responsible Self* (N.Y.: Harper and Row, 1963), p. 71.
[22] W.C. Spohn, *"The Reasoning Heart,"* p. 36.

The corporate belief of a community seems to provide the necessary matrix for the emergence of specific behavior and actions. The behavior and decisions of an individual Christian result from an emergence from within the Christian tradition that necessarily influences questions of ethics and morality. To use an ecological image: ethics is conditioned by its environment. While that environment is manifold, interpersonal, social, ecclesial, as immediate and specific it is the Christian community. The Church must be considered as matrix of faith and of ethics—the *ecclesia* with its life/world-altering message, a distinctive complex of symbols and a distinctive kind of intersubjectivity.

As Spohn writes: "Christian conversion involves moral transformation precisely because it challenges the central images of the self. *Metanoia* means rethinking my personal history through a new set of images which the community proposes as normative."[23]

As an ecclesial discipline, Christian ethics is essentially hermeneutical. It does not begin with a set of a prioris, either philosophical or dogmatic, nor with an unmediated experience; it begins with a collective memory lived and handed down in an ecclesial community. In a hermeneutical theology, understanding can never be the product of the individual's autobiographical reflection alone. Inherited knowledge constitutes the framework in which an individual perceives and experiences. The ecclesial communities are in Ghislain LaFont's words:

> at once theological place and hermeneutical place. They are the former because if the conduct and the objectives which define a community are in conformity with the Gospel in a given situation they deliver by themselves something of the evangelical message which can be read and revealed only there. They are a hermeneutical place because the objective gift of faith is never perceived except from the angle from which each of the communities, in fact, receives and lives it.[24]

To insist on the role of tradition is to establish the need for hermeneutics in Christian ethics. Tradition can be defined as experiences

---

[23]Ibid., p. 35.
[24]Ghislain LaFont, "Monastic Life and Theological Stories," *Monastic Studies* 12 (1976), p. 1.

which are handed down; and as such, traditions according to Schillebeeckx "are at the same time a means of objectifying new experiences and integrating them in what has already been attained."[25] "Experience is traditional experience: experience and tradition are therefore not opposite *per se;* they make one another possible—even new experiences are possible only within the sphere of a tradition."[26] The necessity of hermeneutics is posed by the nature of human experience. Experience is interpretative, and again according to Schillebeeckx, "Interpretation also makes experiencing possible; the authority of experience is therefore *from* experiences and *for* new experiences.

The hermeneutical nature of Christian ethics has serious implications for the truth claims and universal claims of the Christian tradition. While these two claims cannot be separated, they are different in nature and give rise to different problems.

From a hermeneutical perspective, I am suggesting that the fundamental issue in the question of the specificity of Christian ethics can only be addressed by an historical description of how and in what way the reception of Jesus Christ as fundamental and foundational to faith has been effective in the making of the Christian *humanum*. In affirming this we are positing a hermeneutical circle which impedes us from separating too radically interpretation from correlation. Jesus Christ interprets for Christians the meaning of humanity, yet he is recognized as a model and revelation of authentic humanity because Christians, as women and men sharing in a common humanity, bring to this acknowledgment an idea of authentic humanity derived from their own participation in human existence.

Because of the very nature of tradition its truth-claims cannot be concerned solely with original foundations, but with ongoing reception, development and praxis. Because of the nature of tradition itself, the question of truth and meaning cannot be addressed only to foundations or fundamental principles, but to the many and diverse elements constitutive of a tradition. In attempting to get to the truth and meaning of a tradition, a hermeneutic of reception is necessary; a pure method of correlation is not workable. As Fiorenza writes, "The danger of the method

---

[25] Edward Schillebeeckx, *Christ, The Experience of Jesus as Lord* (N.Y.: Crossroad Press, 1980), p. 38.
[26] Ibid.

of correlation, understood as the correlation between relation and the cognitional and normative claims of the modern world consists, in the risk of positing one of the two elements (here revelation and common human experience) as foundational."[27] Correlation is a basic dynamic of tradition itself; experience is always constituted by and is constitutive of tradition.

Meaning in tradition is mediated by symbols appropriate to the tradition. Many of these symbols are idiosyncratic and intelligible only from within a specific tradition—yet there are symbols shared by all cultures which carry the same or at least similar meanings for large segments, if not for all of humankind.

One can speak about "anthropological constants."[28] E. Schillebeeckx, in presenting these constants, discerns three planes within the historical process which interpenetrate one another and constitute one history. The first plane is constituted by the events of everyday life as they come and go. This is called a "fact-constituted history." The second plane is more of an interpretative one. It implies a given intellectual horizon and has a more profound import. Schillebeeckx called this plane "conjunctural history." The last plane is understood as a "structural history." It is made up of historical yet basic structures which change very slowly, structures that have "stationary depth."

Between the last two planes of history there is an on-going dialectical tension. According to Schillebeeckx, it is this tension in particular that makes each history ambivalent and makes imperative an on-going process of interpretation, which is also a process of discovery. Basic structures are not simply given; they are also to be brought about. It cannot simply be stated that history has dissolved our ability to decide moral questions by appealing to the finality of our human nature or to the revelation of God's will in the person of Jesus Christ. The failure of a foundationist and transcendent approach to philosophy and theology does not necessarily lead us to an absolute relativism.

---

[27]F. Schüssler Fiorenza, *Foundational Theology: Jesus and the Church* (New York: Crossroad, 1984), p. 303.

[28]The term 'anthropological constants' is employed by Peter Berger and Thomas Luckmann in *The Social Construction of Reality: A Treatise in the Sociology of Knowledge* (Garden City: Doubleday, 1967) p. 49. Edward Schillebeeckx attempts a presentation of seven such constants in his book *Christ*, op. cit., pp. 731–743.

To affirm the existence of a specific Christian ethics within the cultural perspective we established in no way leads to imperialism or exclusiveness. It is a false dilemma to affirm that becoming human is, for Christians, a prior matter to becoming Christian. Clearly, the goal is that of becoming human. For the Christian, the way to becoming human is the Christian way. It is an error to think that we can come into an unmediated identification with the human community. Identity, human or Christian, is always a relational matter; it is always a social question involving the mediation of communities, in our case the Christian community. That it is the only way to humanization is a theological claim that has no foundation in the facticity of history.

The claim to a specific Christian ethics, though, does imply that a specifically Christian canon can and ought to have primacy over other sources of moral wisdom for the believer. This in no way implies that other sources are not valuable or are simply confirmative of what is already present within the Christian canon. Nor does canonicity imply that the move from the particular to the universal is necessary or that it is impossible. Canonicity is as historical as everything else; in no way does it eliminate the pluralistic context of the moral agent, Christian or other.

The Christian narrative is certainly paradigmatic for the moral identity of a Christian individual. A canon functions evaluatively in ethical reflection. This does not imply a priori that these values will never be rationally persuasive to all rational human beings. There is nothing wrong in saying in a non-proselytizing way that the Bible belongs to the world. As James Barr writes:

> When the Church addresses the world on the basis of the Bible, it invites people to look for themselves and see if these things are not so. The possibility that people may do this looking for themselves carries with it a consequence on the more scholarly level: non-Christian interpretation of the Bible is a possibility, indeed it is more, it is a reality."[29]

The acceptance of a specific Christian ethics should not lead to the denial of the existence of transcultural reality to human existence and its meaning. It simply affirms that there is a transcultural reality of the hu-

---

[29] James Barr, *Old and New Interpretation* (N.Y.: Harper and Row, 1966), p. 191.

man self, however finite any specific understanding of the reality may be. As Thomas Ogletree writes:

> Thus, though there is a structure to moral understanding which is derived from constitutive features of the human way of being in the world, that structure always appears concretely in forms and modes which are relative to a given history with its unique experiences and its distinctive cultural legacy.[30]

Within this cross-cultural understanding of Christian ethics, George Lindbeck's cultural-linguistic theory of religion and religious language is helpful.[31]

It is Lindbeck's claim that the best way to do justice to a religious tradition is to engage in "thick description" of the actual behavior, processes and communication that take place in a tradition.[32] A cultural-linguistic approach, while favoring a "hermeneutic of retrieval," is not incompatible with a hermeneutic of suspicion. Nor does a cultural-linguistic approach to religious traditions necessarily lead to some kind of sociological sectarianism, i.e. small communal enclaves. This is not to

---

[30] Thomas Ogletree, *The Use of the Bible in Christian Ethics* (Philadelphia: Fortress Press, 1983) p. 36.

[31] Religion is, according to Lindbeck: "a kind of cultural and/or linguistic framework or medium which shapes the entirety of life and thought. It functions somewhat like a Kantian **a priori**, although in this case the **a priori** is a set of acquired skills which could be different. It is not primarily an array of beliefs about the true and the good (though it may involve these), nor a symbolism expressive of basic attitudes, feelings or sentiments (though these will be generated). Rather, it is similar to an idiom which makes possible the description of realities, the formulation of beliefs, and the experiencing of inner attitudes, feelings and sentiments. Like a culture or language, it is a communal phenomenon which shapes the subjectivities of individuals rather than being primarily a manifestation of those subjectivities. It comprises a vocabulary of discursive and non-discursive symbols together with a distinctive logic or grammar in terms of which this vocabulary can be meaningfully deployed. Lastly, just as a language (or "language game" to use Wittgenstein's phrase) is correlated with a form of life, and just as a culture has both cognitive and behavioral dimensions, so also in the case of a religious tradition. Its doctrines, cosmic stories or myths, and ethical directives are integrally related to the rituals it practices, the sentiments or experiences it evokes, the actions it recommends, and the institutional forms it develops." George A. Lindbeck, *The Nature of Doctrine, Religion and Theology in a Postliberal Age* (Philadelphia: The Westminster Press, 1984), p. 33.

[32] Ibid., p. 115.

misunderstand the importance of small communities. Harvey Cox's recent *Religion in the Secular City*[33] finds in the disciplined communities of liberation theology and fundamentalism hope for the future of Christianity. Some of the basic questions being asked today are about the process to be used in making meaningful moral discourse within the larger society. Clearly the answer cannot be simply an either/or: concern only for common discourse or the specific language of a "small communal enclave."

The cultural-linguistic approach simply affirms a more empirical understanding of religious tradition. In criticizing the more transcendental approach of Rahner, Lindbeck writes:

> When one pictures inner experiences as prior to expression and communication, it is natural to think of them in their most basic and elemental form as also prior to conceptualization. If, in contrast, expressive and communicative symbol systems, whether linguistic or nonlinguistic, are primary—then, while there are of course nonreflective experiences, there are no uninterpreted or unschematized ones. On this view, the means of communication and expression are a precondition, a kind of quasi-transcendental (i.e., culturally formed) **a priori** for the possibility of experience. We cannot identify, describe, or recognize experience qua experience without the use of signs and symbols.[34]

The cultural-linguistic approach does not necessarily imply that the language of a religion is exempt from critical assessment from all perspectives other than its own.[35] If this were the case it would simply mean that the same person and community have two very different ways of construing the reality of life in the world side by side.

The truth claims of a tradition even from a cultural-linguistic approach need not be ignored nor are they primarily subjective truths. It is not necessary to choose between concern for the truth claims and plau-

---

[33] Harvey Cox, *Religion in the Secular City. Toward a Postmodern Theology* (N.Y.: Simon and Schuster, 1984).

[34] G. Lindbeck, *The Nature of Doctrine*, op..cit. p. 38.

[35] cf. Paul Holmer, *The Grammar of Faith* (N.Y.: Harper and Row, 1978), pp. 63 ff.

sibility claims of a religious tradition and a defense of the Christian tradition.

According to the cultural-linguistic approach, it is necessary to have the means for expressing an experience in order to have it, and the richer our expressive or linguistic system, the more subtle, varied and differentiated can be our experience. A religious tradition and its doctrines are the means for expressing and therefore for experiencing and knowing. But the tradition is also constituted by handed-down experiences.

While for Lindbeck, the truth and meaning of a tradition is essentially intratextual, a cultural-linguistic approach is not incompatible with the possibility and even the necessity of "extra-textual" meaning and truth. In fact, without such external reference, choosing a Christian identity or one form of life over another would be purely arbitrary.

It is Christianity's claim that the Christian identity, while particular and historical in nature, has universal value and implications. In fact, the search for a universal normative horizon of meaning for human history—an horizon having normative implications for present and future practice—is necessary for the publicness of any ethics. For ethics can never be simply a selective interpretation and rationalization of the past. Ethics in its essential work is an evaluative hermeneutic of history. Without a claim to some universal validity Christians cannot maintain a conviction of the truth of their faith and message; "for," as W. Pannenberg writes, "a truth that would be simply my truth and would not at least claim to be universal and valid for every human being could not remain true even for me."[36]

There is a conviction within Christianity that a connection exists between its basic religious symbols and general human morality; that these symbols provide a truthful understanding of God, self and the world. Within Christianity there is a general conviction that in its foundational narratives and texts one is encountered by the revelation of a deeper dimension of the "universally human fact." Yet the challenge to Christianity's claim to universal truth comes from Christianity itself with its emphasis on the particular and the historical. And with the emergence of an historical-critical consciousness, we have become increasingly

---

[36] Wolfhart Pannenberg, *Anthropology in Theological Perspective* (Philadelphia: Westminster Press, 1985), p. 15.

aware of the historically contingent starting point of the Christian faith. We do not know the full historical truth about Jesus nor do we know how to get to that truth. Thus we are still haunted by Lessing's question of whether it is possible to stake our existence and ultimate purpose on a historically contingent starting point.

The discussion of Christian ethics brings home to us the importance of the historical and contingent, and the need for universality. It is not possible simply to imprison Christian communities in their historical particularity depriving them of their basis and their human legitimacy, or preventing them from allowing for the irreducible finitude of *human beings* and *crushing* them under the deadly requirement of a uniformity which denies differences. True universality is the result of conquest and not a starting point; it is not easily realizable.

For Christian ethics, as for Christian theology, there is a necessary detour to universality via a tradition. There is even a necessity for conversion; there is a need to attend and listen—to commit oneself. Christian ethics is linked to a tradition; it becomes a factuality and a history with its texts and its institutional concretions. Yet the necessity of a detour through tradition does not simply render concern for the universal illegitimate. What is important is the process by which one attempts to arrive at the universal.

Not only is the process to be carefully chosen, but the very question of the nature of the universal needs to be examined. One must not think of the universal in terms of extension where the real could be comprehended by thought. To talk in terms of extension or of totalization is to believe that reality, including humanity, can be circumscribed and dominated by an expression of the essential. It is necessary to modify universality to absolute; not particular and universal but particular and absolute. Absolute in Christian ethics is not a concept of extension but of in-tension; what is needed is not a journey of extension but of intensification. For at the core of Christian ethics lies a person.

Knowledge in Christian ethics is linked not only to a particular framework, but also to a particular person, Jesus Christ. The object of the journey from the particular to the "universal" is the "universal" significance of Jesus Christ. That "universal" significance may well be eschatological in nature, more like an axis applicable to history rather than a reality easily realizable within history itself.

The "person" of Jesus Christ is mediated to us through the tradition. The process of intensification demands a willingness to dwell in and with the tradition.[37] Grasping the "universal significance" of Jesus Christ will be the consequence of standing within a happening of tradition rather than the product of any particular method of inquiry ethical or theological.

When dealing with religious traditions, one is confronted with the diversity of religious traditions, the variety of cultural codes—each claiming to have the truth. When religious traditions are perceived from within a historical/critical consciousness, it is difficult to avoid some form of relativism. For certain forms of historical consciousness all cultures and traditions are assumed to possess equal status and validity, for there are no scientific categories capable of rating or hermeneutically evaluating cultures or religious traditions. Within that context then, the question must be asked about how communicable religious traditions are, how intelligible they can be to those outside the tradition, and how much certitude they can generate for their adherents in order to withstand competitive claims. In this situation there must be a concern, as J. Gustafson states, "for the intellectual and moral life of the Christian community, its credibility and its capacities to deal with alternative construals of life without retreating into intellectual and moral sectarianism."[38]

A successful tradition must have credibility, intelligibility, authority—and the means for affirmation and renewal of itself. A theory of tradition must take these various aspects into account in its development. What has been proposed is a theory based on a linguistic model for communication. According to R. Schreiter, "since communication maintenance and management of information are central concerns of tradition, the model recommends itself as a possibility."[39] Faith and tradition are analogous to language.[40]

---

[37]Cf. E. Schillebeeckx, *Jesus*, op. cit., pp. 573–611.

[38]J. Gustafson, "Response to Critics," *Journal of Religious Ethics*, vol. 13, Number 2 Fall 1985, p. 187.

[39]R. Schreiter, *Constructing Local Theologies*, op. cit., p. 114.

[40][Let] "us apply this model to the problem of Christian tradition. Tradition is analogous to the entire language system. Faith is analogous to language competence. Theology and the expressive tradition (liturgy, wider forms of praxis) are analogous to language performance. The loci of orthodoxy (however construed: Scriptures, creeds, councils, confes-

One of the interesting aspects of this theory is its application to the question of orthodoxy or of identity.[41]

The loci of orthodoxy are primarily the basic and fundamental texts and their official interpreters. These loci do not create theology for any community. Again, according to Schreiter:

> The loci of orthodoxy, like grammar, undergo transformation as performance texts (local-theology texts) change. Thus condemnations of heresy can be lifted or forgotten when circumstances have changed (one thinks of the Galileo case in Roman Catholicism).[42]

From within this theory tradition can be perceived as the equivalent of a language system. According to Schreiter,

> Tradition is more than unarticulated faith, but it includes that. Tradition is more than the loci of orthodoxy, but it includes that. And tradition is more than the history of theology, but includes that. Without the competence of faith, the loci of orthodoxy are barren. Without the performance texts of communities, Christianity is mute.[43]

The influence and importance of ethics within a tradition is intrinsically linked to a constant, ongoing mutuality of lived faith and orthodoxy. Commitment to truth, justice and charity is essential to the tradition's discovery of the meaning of its own vision. The praxis of a tradition is not simply a warrant that discloses the truth of its vision but it is also a source of the discovery of such meaning and truth. A Christian's way of being in the world is hermeneutical; there is a constant need to respond and to convert. Liberation theology has made the point again that what Christians do is essential to who Christians are. The meaning

---

sions, magisterium) represent a grammar, mediating competence and performance." Ibid., p. 115.

[41] "And just as grammar is more successful in determining what is not a well-formed phrase than what is always a well-formed phrase, so too the loci of orthodoxy, even though sometimes positive in formulation, are really negative or delimiting in function. Creedal formulas set boundaries on belief but do not attempt to describe all possible combinations within those boundaries." Ibid., p. 116.

[42] Ibid.

[43] Ibid.

of a tradition's vision can come to be known through Christian performance; credibility and plausibility are measured in terms of performance. This does not eliminate the fact that in the relation between truth claims and practice claims must be a relation between the ideal and the actual. The ethical significance of Christianity's convictions depends on the power of those convictions to shape a moral community. Tradition implies the necessity for witnessing and for discipleship. Christian discipleship redefines the standards of morality in a distinctively Christian direction by locating them in paradigmatic texts and symbols of the Christian tradition. In some way we need to look to specific persons to weigh the value of competing stories. To some extent, each story is the kind of person it shapes.

Within the emphasis on discipleship and witnessing the more classical natural law tension between a universal norm and a concrete situation is replaced by an eschatological tension between a humanity on the way and the present human condition. The emphasis and importance given to discipleship and witnessing is now severely tested by the situation in which most religious traditions find themselves.[44]

In a hermeneutical ethics there is no one response, "no single journey of recognition and expression of the Christ-event . . . Rather each theologian finds some elective affinity between some interpretation of the questions and responses of the Christian tradition and hence of the Christ-event."[45]

What is implied here is that Christians are invited to commitment to a relative "essence." This is no easy stance since it demands that an individual move beyond the explicit ideological systems and clear boundaries of identity. James Fowler describes this stance as conjunctive faith. According to Fowler:

---

[44] According to J. Cahill, "In the developed societies of the West stability and reliability are not striking characteristics of the traditional religions. The environment in which tradition exists has been altered; there are competitors in the world of meaning. There are disagreements within the traditions themselves as to what is constitutive and what is consequent. The confirmatory force of the environment is diminished or lacking. Transmitters of the tradition are somewhat less than convinced of its efficacy. And there are still cases of the propagation of unhealthy systems that appeal to the unfortunate and sick strata of society. Therefore the vehicles of transmission manifest a certain impotence in normal circumstances." J. Cahill, *Mended Speech,* op. cit., p. 68.

[45] David Tracy, *The Analogical Imagination* (N.Y.: Crossroad, 1981), p. 323.

This position implies no lack of commitment to one's own tradition. Nor does it mean a wishy-washy neutrality or mere fascination with the exotic features of alien cultures. Rather conjunctive faith's radical openness to the truth of the other systems stems precisely from its confidence in the reality mediated by its own tradition and in the awareness that reality overspills its mediation.[46]

The awareness of the relativity of all our own constructs and interpretations frees us from the illusion of control and enables us to appreciate more fully the truth and relativity of past interpretations. As John Cobb writes: " . . . the more deeply we trust Christ, the more openly receptive we will be to wisdom from any source, and the more responsibly critical we will be both of our own received habits of mind and of the limitations and distortions of others."[47]

The awareness of the relativity of our traditional constructs and yet the necessity of a journey of intensification demands that the tradition that can be trusted and that can nurture one's ethical identity must be such that it permits authentic pluralism. Vatican II in its "Declaration on Religious Liberty" affirms:

> . . . everybody has the duty and consequently the right to seek the truth in religious matters so that, through the use of appropriate means, he may prudently form judgments of conscience which are sincere and true.
>
> The search for truth, however, must be carried out in a manner that is appropriate to the dignity of the human person and his social nature, namely, by free enquiry with the help of teaching or instruction, communication and dialogue. It is by these means that men share with each other the truth they have discovered, or think they have discovered, in such a way that they help one another in the search for truth. Moreover, it is by personal assent that men must adhere to the truth they have discovered.[48]

That search for truth can only be possible in a faith-community that allows and fosters authentic dialogue.

---

[46] James Fowler, *Stages of Faith* (N.Y.: Harper and Row, 1981), p. 107.

[47] John Cobb, "The Religious" in *Christian Theology*, Peter Hodgson, ed. (Philadelphia: Fortress Press, 1982), p. 319.

[48] *Dignitatis Humanae*, in *Vatican Council II*, p. 801.

True dialogue does not invade; it does not manipulate. For there can be no such thing as dialogical manipulation. The primary dimension of true dialogue is intersubjectivity, or intercommunication, which cannot be reduced to a simple relation between a knowing subject and a knowable object. Just as there is no such thing as an isolated human being there is also no such thing as isolated thinking.

The very nature of the ecclesial community as an interpretative community requires an appreciation of the significance of lives different from its members' lives. Its catholicity should not be the result of a monolithic uniformity but the fruit of communication and communion. In fact the paradigm of dialogical communication is central for setting the conditions for adequate public moral discourse. The ethical content of a tradition need not impose itself with a nature-like compulsion. The opposite of a nature-like compulsion of norms is a mutual agreement on norms, reached in a free reciprocal process of communication. The development of a tradition and the journey of intensification within a tradition can and in fact should be conceived as communicative competence: within a tradition individuals need to become competent to test and render perspicuous for one another assertions and behavioral expectations through a linguistically mediated process of reciprocal reflectivity. Such a dialogue, contrary to Habermas,[49] is not contrary to a prior commitment to a tradition; but it does demand the willingness to be encountered and challenged, which is, in fact, the reason for the existence of the Christian tradition itself.

An historical community is paradigmatic for the moral identity of the individual who identifies with this community. No dichotomy can be established between the Church and its mission and the specificity of ethics. In order to arrive at an adequate perception of what a Christian ethics is or should be, there is need for an interpretation of Christian identity. An ethics which has to develop in the context of historicity and hermeneutics must ask itself what is constitutive in its own tradition and what is consequent.

According to F. Fiorenza,

---

[49]Cf. Jurgen Habermas, *Communication and the Evolution of Society* trans. Thomas McCarthy. (Boston: Beacon Press, 1976).

> This task is not an easy task, for although Christianity and Christian traditions are historically and empirically given, Christian identity is not. It is given only as the result of an interpretative reconstruction of the tradition in its past and present forms of existence.[50]

To arrive at a workable understanding of Christian identity, there must be more than a descriptive analysis of various stages of development of a tradition; there must be a critical discernment of what is essential or accidental, of what is authentic and what is not. Here, a hermeneutic of reception is not satisfied with simply looking at foundations but must take "as its basis the considered judgments of Christians, both present and past, as to what constitutes the Christian vision in its beliefs and practices and seeks to uncover an identity in the midst of diversity."[51]

Such a process or method presupposes that the starting point in the attempt to arrive at a workable concept of Christian identity is not "a transcendental a priori or a phenomenological analysis of abstract structures of possibility, but rather the historical manifestation of the religious dimension of life as it is exhibited in a particular religious tradition."[52] These manifestations are thoroughly historical; they evolve, change, have consequences and effects.

Such a consideration of the tradition relative to the construction of a workable understanding of Christian identity is critical

> in that it has the task of bringing to the fore the identity of the tradition as it exists in the paradigmatic ideals, both in theory and practice, of the tradition. These paradigms provide criteria for evaluating certain developments as legitimate and others as deformations.[53]

A workable Christian identity expressed in a complex of symbols, models and paradigms must have the capacity to illuminate experience and praxis; such a capacity functions as a warrant for the tradition.

---

[50] F. Schüssler Fiorenza, *Foundational Theology: Jesus and the Church*, op. cit., p. 304.
[51] Ibid.
[52] Ibid., p. 305.
[53] Ibid., p. 306.

V.

Christian Identity and Christian Ethics

Christian ethics and Christian identity are intimately related. And while Christian identity is not simply a given but must be hammered out by every generation of Christians, it is not an identity without parameters. In Paul's letter to the Philippians (2:5), Christians are invited: "Let this be the disposition that governs in your common life, as is fitting in Christ Jesus." Paul is not presenting Christ as the ethical ideal for our imitation. He is presenting, especially in the hymn that follows the initiation, the Paschal Mystery as the ground of the ethical appeal, the fact of the redemptive victory which Christ has won.

The Paschal Mystery is a complex of symbols, the center of which is the person of Jesus Christ. The Paschal Mystery was an attempt to bring to expression the manifestation of God in Jesus Christ. This God is a God who makes a difference in our lives, and the difference is the person of Jesus Christ.

The God of Jesus Christ, the God revealed in Jesus Christ, cannot be thought of at all unless the idea irritates and encroaches. Thinking about such a God implies a review of interests and needs that are directly related to ourselves: conversion and exodus form part of the basic structure of such thinking.

Essential to the meaning of the Paschal Mystery is its embodiment in praxis. As Langdon Gilkey writes of the religious symbols,

> They promise illumination, a new understanding. They challenge the way we concretely are. They call for a new way of being, a new at-

titude to ourselves and to others, new forms of our actual relations in community, and a new kind of action in the world . . . every fundamental theological symbol means a critical stance toward past and present forms of existence and order in the social world, and the call to historical and social action on behalf of a new earth.[1]

The other side of this affirmation is the realization that false concepts of God generate or provide fertile ground for the dehumanization and distortion of human life. If Christian ethical discourse is to advance the task of developing an adequate evaluative-hermeneutic of the true, the right, and the good, substantial critical reconstructive work relative to the Paschal Mystery and therefore to the conceptualizations of the person of Jesus Christ is needed.

For Christianity, the decisive symbol is Jesus as the Christ. Christianity cannot understand itself, direct its actions, or give form to its conduct without the use of the symbol Jesus Christ. It is the interpretation of this symbol that is problematic in the debate on the distinctiveness of Christian ethics. It is problematic because of fundamental claims made about Jesus Christ.

Christianity proclaims that in Christ the human ideal for which all persons strive has been attained in history and, in fact, that unless one be human as Christ was human, one cannot be human at all. Jesus Christ is not only the revelation of God, but also the revelation of humanness. In him the questions as to who is God and who is human are answerable only in their complementarity not as two questions but as one.

Within the Christian context, God's revealing and redemptive presence and action in the world is believed to be paradigmatically expressed in the person of Jesus Christ. The Christian is invited to find in Jesus Christ *the* focal interpretative symbol for the understanding of divine activity in nature, history and society. Whether one speaks about God's causal relation to the world, about the morality and authenticity of human action and behavior, or about the basic sources for understanding ethics, the one underlying context is always Christological. In a sense, Christianity is characterized by bipolarity: it is governed by two logics: one which relates the life of the believer to God and the other which

---

[1]Langdon Gilkey, *Naming the Whirlwind: The Renewal of God Language* (Indianapolis: Bobbs-Merrill, 1969), p. 464.

orders it around faith in Jesus the Christ. For in the teaching of the New Testament, we have the affirmation that Christ is the unique embodiment of the purposive, restorative, creating self-expression of God and God's will for communion with God's creation. Bipolarity is probably not the best term to characterize the tension inherent to Christianity. The word "contrapletal" is a better way of expressing what appears as a bipolarity in Christianity. What is suggested by this term is that while the poles appear and in some sense are over against (contra) each other, yet each needs the other for a statement of the complete truth. What is contrapletal is not simply dialectical because there is no necessity to choose between the poles and it does not proceed through thesis and antithesis to a synthesis that would simply gather up the poles into a distinctively new reality. In a "contrapletal" situation, there is no necessity to choose one pole over the other, God or Jesus Christ, but both can be chosen yet with their proper inner dimensions.

In order to avoid a false bipolarity in Christianity as the collapsing of either pole, God or Jesus Christ, one needs a "contrapletal" Christology. That task is no easy one considering the polarization or false synthesis that has taken place between the human and the divine, between Being and Becoming, the eternal and the temporal, creation and redemption.

A contrapletal Christology is one that, by necessity, must integrate the Christian doctrines of Creation, Incarnation and Redemption. The greatest obstacle to such an integration is the basic dichotomy that has emerged between the creation of this world and the redemption of this world.

The doctrine of creation has become an obvious and central concern of theology today. The reason for this basic change can be found in the area of soteriology and the emphasis on salvation as occurring **in** this world. As Douglas Hall writes:

> So long as redemption theology is content to explore the prospects of an ultimate salvific state transcending this world, the doctrine of creation holds at best a secondary interest for Christians; and since the tendency towards otherworldliness in redemption theory has never been *very* far away from the heart of Christian discourse and spirituality, creation in much traditional doctrine and liturgy has almost seemed the very thing that had to be overcome—a sort of failed ex-

periment of the deity, incapable of being righted, thus leaving rescue from it the only alternative.[2]

Yet the general experience of the deep wrongness of our world leads many to ask about the possible redemption of *this* world. What should this world be?

This question cannot be answered outside of a doctrine of creation, for creation as a doctrine of faith and not a scientific theory intends to affirm belief in the nature and goal of creaturely life; it is there to help discern what is essential and what is intended. In a Christian context the question about the purpose of this world, and its redemption cannot be separated from the belief in and the doctrine of the person of Christ. The integration of a doctrine of redemptive Incarnation and Creation necessitates a process of reinterpretation of the doctrines of Creation, Incarnation and Redemption. In this reinterpretation, the basic and fundamental problematic of the specificity of Christian ethics will be addressed.

The question and the problem of the specificity of Christian ethics is one of the most difficult questions Christian theology has to answer at a theoretical as well as a practical level, because it is on this question that important areas of theology coalesce and appear more problematic. The nature of Christian ethics is the major test for the Church's claim to a universal vocation as witness to the salvation of all in Jesus Christ. It is a claim that should not lead to a false Christian universality nor to the encouragement of forms of intolerance and domination.

While a major emphasis has been given to Church and Tradition in the question of specific Christian ethics, the major problematic area is that of Christology. In fact, Christology is the most critical doctrinal issue for any aspect of Christian theology. Every attempt to formulate an adequate Christology is substantially determined by the various issues theologians and ecclesial communities face in particular times and places. Conflicts relative to Christology are not simply about what was said of Jesus in Scripture or in Tradition.

In the debate on the specificity of Christian ethics, the question cen-

---

[2]Douglas Hall, *God and Human Suffering. An Exercise in the Theology of the Cross* (Minneapolis: Augsburg Publishing House, 1986), pp. 49–50.

ters on the revelatory and transformative claims made relative to the person of Jesus Christ. The basic question becomes: Is Jesus Christ the exclusive medium of human liberation? Is Christ indispensable to the process of attaining proper human freedom? What is the nature of what Christ has done for us? What does our believing in him do for us? Does Jesus Christ function in a unique way in empowering the moral life? After the coming of Christ, how much of the "human" is still left unknown and is still to be discovered? Is there a "humanness" outside the humanness of Jesus Christ? One only has to recall certain texts from Vatican II: " . . . Christ the Lord, the new Adam, in the very revelation of the mystery of the Father and of his love, fully reveals man to himself and brings to light his most high calling."[3]

"Missionary activity is intimately bound up with human nature and its aspirations. In manifesting Christ, the Church reveals to men their true situation and calling, since Christ is the head and exemplar of that renewed humanity. . . ."[4]

Again, the question presses itself upon us: How is it possible to claim that Christianity as an historical religion can lay hold of every person as the sole mediator of the relationship to the absolute? This claim appears excessive, especially as one moves in the realm of ethics: public moral discussion demands general participation while specific religious traditions concern particular individuals with particular beliefs.

Our emphasis on the necessary role of tradition relative to Christian ethics implies a limitation on Christianity's claims for universality.[5] The traditionary process is essentially historical and social; in the realm of ethics as in other realms, it functions primarily through a process of socialization. Whatever universality or absoluteness any tradition claims for itself will necessarily be qualified; such universality or absoluteness will necessarily have its point of departure within the particular. Whatever the nature of Christ's transforming power is, it will necessarily be historical and social in nature; whatever faith and belief are, they do not escape the process of socialization. Whatever difference a Christian ethic makes, it cannot contradict human ethics or go beyond the human. While

---

[3] *Gaudium et Spes,* No. 22, p. 922.
[4] *Ad Gentes,* No. 8, p. 822.
[5] cf. A.E. Harvey, *Jesus and the Constraints of History* (Philadelphia: Westminster Press, 1982).

faith and grace are the decisive elements in a Christian anthropology, the question still remains, and again, it is basically a Christological one, "What do they add to ethics?" Certainly they are not something that goes beyond the human, for there cannot be any radical discontinuity between the human and the Christian. There is an inescapable concreteness of the experience of grace and faith—an inescapable historicality and sociality.[6]

The incarnation or embodiment of unlimited subjectivity which faith and grace claim to lead to, always has quite concrete economic, social, political and cultural locations. Unlimited subjectivity is always contextual; it is shared subjectivity—ecclesial subjectivity. Grace and faith are realized in history and society; here rather than there; in this situation rather than that; now rather than then. The differences implied here do not affect only matters that are external and peripheral, but the realization in a concrete body of human beings of those distinctive meanings and values centered on the figure of Jesus Christ.

The basic question relative to the specificity of Christian ethics becomes that of the nature of the religious versus the human. Within Christianity this becomes a question about Christology, for in Christianity Jesus Christ is believed to have experienced what it is to be related to God and what it is to be human in the fullest and deepest way. In Jesus Christ God is fully revealed and present, as is humanity's humanness. The Constitution *Gaudium et Spes* underlines that aspect, constantly and pressingly presenting Jesus Christ as the "new man" and the true answer to the mystery of human destiny.

While Christology has been and still is the most critical doctrinal issue for Christian theology, the theology of creation must be given a greater critical importance. In reexamining the doctrine and symbols of creation, it is necessary to look again at the meaning of *ex nihilo*. This, in turn, will oblige us to review our understanding of God as creator and ourselves as creatures.

The doctrine of *creatio ex nihilo* shocked the Greek mind since it was understood as anchoring the world in instability or flux. From the metaphysical immutability of God one had to move into the historical

---

[6]cf. Roger Haight S.J., *The Experience and Language of Grace* (N.Y.: Paulist Press, 1979).

fidelity of God—the covenantal God. It moved toward the eruption of history and of a world as an open-ended reality in movement toward a yet unknown future. There is a movement away from the closed predeterminism of Aristotle, and the changeless natural world of the Stoics. Within the concept of creation as originated in Hebrew thought and in Christianity, there is, according to Torrance, an "astonishing combination of unpredictability and lawfulness, not only in the history of man but in the history of all created reality in its relation to the constancy and freedom of the grace of the creator that lies behind Christian conception of the cosmos as an open-ordered universe."[7] The universe's origination from God is characterized neither by uncertainty nor by necessity; it is neither closed nor predetermined, but open to novel and unknown forms. This implies that the created universe is not centered on itself but in relation to God as transcendent creator; but it is to be ultimately completed by this same creator. While the world is dependent upon God in a radical way, it is also a distinctive reality other than God and reflected in its otherness.

In the priestly tradition the expression "create" is used in connection with the creation of human beings (Gen. 1:27). What distinguishes this creation from the creation of other realities is that human beings are created in the image of God. As image of God, human beings are the mirror of God. The creation of man/woman as image of God and therefore the nature of God's immanence to God's creation, necessitates a further elaboration of the nature of creation "ex nihilo."

While creating is an act of emanation from God, one has to affirm the radical transcendence of God. Creation is not identical with the being of God, nor is it a part of God's being; it is not *homoousios* with God. Creation is brought into being without adding to or subtracting from the being of God; and yet God is not absent from God's creation.

The non-absence of God from creation raises issues such as the relation of the immanence of God to God's transcendence and the nature of God's agency. The absolute and radical transcendence of God even as creator does not necessarily lead us to an apathetic God, but to pure liberality. In fact, only a God who, as Being itself, is absolutely transcendent and independent of the world can give in pure graciousness,

---

[7] T. F. Torrance, *Divine and Contingent Order* (Oxford: Oxford Press, 1981), p. 69.

since by giving God does not gain any benefit for himself. The absolute dependence of the creature simply conveys the truth that all things come from God.

Transcendence must qualify and characterize God in every aspect. As agent God is total agency, complete self-giving, utter generosity of sharing; in God nothing is held back, nothing is given by measure. The trinitarian nature of God indicates this. Yet in creation the gift has to be limited if there is a passing from the infinite to the finite. How can the infinite, which is infinite giving, give less than itself, give less than the infinite? Does the very nature of the infinite exclude "otherness"? In the context of trinitarian doctrine the answer must be negative. Yet the "otherness" here is also "sameness." In God there are three persons and only one substance. What about "otherness" that is not "sameness?" Does infinite being exclude all ek-stasis, all going beyond itself? Or does it imply rather the fullness of this generosity?

In the Christian context the nature of our God must be found in the statement that "he who seeks to save himself must lose himself" (Matt. 16:25). The perfection of the divine nature lies not in its infinite self-satisfaction but in its self-giving love.[8] Of course, there is nothing other than God or independent of God to which God can give himself. Yet may not God bring into *being* that which, being other than God, though always dependent upon God, can be the object of God's love and share in God's own nature? The idea of creation as a form of divine self-giving, a love which goes out of itself to bring about fully responsive reality entails that God puts himself at the disposal of creatures and limits himself in relation to them. Creation as ek-stasis is in some real sense a *self-limitation of God*.

Christian theology, in light of the trinitarian mystery, has always distinguished between an act of God inwards and an act of God outwards. It has distinguished between the inner life of God and an act of God outwards, in creation, incarnation, and redemption. If we say that there is a "within" and "without" for God, and that God goes "out of himself" in creating, then we have to accept a self-limitation of the infinite relative to God's creation. In order to create that which is outside

---

[8] The Aristotelian God is the supreme case of self-centered egoism, *noesis noeseos*, finding supreme happiness in self-contemplation, a sort of eternal narcissist.

of himself, there must be within God the possibility of finitude within himself. Through self-limitation God has created the world "in himself," giving it time *in* eternity, finitude *in* God's infinity. Creation is God's act in God and out of God.[9]

There must be a place for finitude in God before God can create that which is other than God. The *nihil* is within God himself. God's creative act is anchored in God's preceding self-restriction.

Creation is an act not of self-expansion but of self-limitation. While it is true that creation does not mean a lessening of the divine life, through creation God does enter a new, limiting relationship. Through creation God brings about an "other" who is free. In creating, God has surrendered God's triumphant self-sufficiency and brought about God's own need. God has done this freely out of love. Because in God's transcendence God is free from the world that has been brought about, God is also radically free for the world.

There is a basic principle of self-limitation, a kenosis that applies to God in relation to finite being. The nature of God's being as personal agent is a letting-be, an enabling to be. Letting-be is also self-giving or self-spending so that God's creative work is a work of love and self-giving. Creation is not so much an exercise of power as it is an exercise of love and generosity, an act of self-limitation.

---

[9] As J. Moltmann writes: "The world process is therefore to be understood as a two-sided one. Every stage in the creation process contains within itself the tension between the light flooding back into God and light that breaks forth from him. In other words, every act outwards is preceded by an act inwards which makes the 'outwards' possible. God, that is to say, continually creates inwards and outwards simultaneously. He creates by withdrawing himself, and because he withdraws himself. Creation in chaos and out of nothing, which is an act of power, is also a self-humiliation on God's part, a lowering of himself into his own impotence. Creation is a work of God's humility and his withdrawal into himself. God acts on himself when he acts creatively. His inward and his outward aspects therefore correspond to one another and mirror one another. His action is grounded in his passion. Jakob Emden is no doubt right when he says that the doctrine of *zimzum* is the only serious attempt ever made to think through the idea of 'creation out of nothing' in a truly theological way. Even if we do not follow the speculations in natural philosophy which developed out of it, the basic idea of this doctrine gives us the chance to think of *the world in God* without falling victims to pantheism, and to see the history of the divine self-humiliation and the history of human freedom in a continual relation of reciprocity." In *The Trinity and the Kingdom: The Doctrine of God*. (N.Y.: Harper and Row, 1981), p. 110.

Creation is never really from nothing, *ex nihilo,* but out of Godself. There is a sacrificial nature to creation; it is intrinsically a self-humbling, self-restraining, self-limiting act. "The creation of heaven and earth," writes S. Bulgakov, " . . . is a voluntary self-diminution, a metaphysical kenosis, with respect to divinity itself."[10] In order to understand how a unique God brings about an other as an other, some dimension of self-limitation must be attributed to God. This is even more the case when the other is given the specific possibility of freedom and personal relation. In creating not only does God allow for the existence of a reality other than himself, but God actually gives a created being the possibility of choosing to respond to the Creator. By giving to creation a measure of independence, namely, the possibility of loving, God limited himself, and in a real way rendered himself vulnerable. Creation is the work of authentic love and is not simply the effortless expression of the divine will. God's creative activity sets no limits to its own self-giving. It seeks constantly to enlarge the "other's" capacity to receive. In creating, God holds nothing back.

Creation may be termed an omnipotent act of God; but this power is not power as we commonly understand it in human affairs. Power is commonly understood as a controlling domination, the control of things, events and other persons. MacGregor writes: "God does not wield power over his creation; on the contrary, he exercises it in the creative act, and the exercise of it is the exercise of his love."[11] God's omnipotence is characterized and marked by the fact that God's power is to be grasped in the same sense that God's power is effective even in apparent weakness. In God power and love are simply the two sides of the same reality. Because God's creative power is the power of love, God's creating is a letting-be. Love does not only allow the other his or her otherness but actually makes it possible and requires it. The desire to be certain of the other, to guarantee the other's response, is in fact a violation of otherness and love. This can amount to little more than an attempt to control and hence to reduce the other to an instrument of one's interests and purposes.

Such an approach to creation implies the radical rejection of extrin-

---

[10]Quoted in G. MacGregor, *He Who Lets Us Be. A Theology of Love* (New York: Seabury Press, 1975), p. 104.

[11]MacGregor, *op. cit.,* p. 25.

sicism. The infinite is immanent in the finite not by absorbing or destroying it but by taking on its finitude and existence. The infinite is in and through the finite, but never identical with it. The mode of God's immanence is not identity, but transcendence. God's transcendence consists in the fact that God does not remove the difference between himself and what is other, but rather accepts the other precisely as different. God frees human beings to be human and the world to be secular. As Kasper writes: "The intensity of creation's independence grows in direct and not inverse ratio to the intensity of God's action."[12]

God is Creator precisely in relation to a created world. To understand fully God as Creator one must modify the Aristotelian notion of God as an unchangeably self-sufficient impassible being. The concept of the impassibility and immutability of God is actually ambiguous. Classically understood it means that God is not moved by anything outside of himself. Yet God is not eternally Creator; God was free to become the Creator. God was not eternally incarnate; God was free to move outside of himself. As John O'Donnell writes:

> The Christian God is not the absolute, the impassible God of classical philosophical theism, rightly rejected by atheists. The Christian God is the God who suffers in time, who enters our history in the event of Jesus Christ. To think of God in the light of this event is to think of a God whose being is in coming. God's coming to man proceeds from his sovereign freedom of overflowing love. In this sense God's coming is grounded in his transcendence. But since God's being itself is his coming, we cannot think of God without his creation or without man. Man is not accidental or external to God but through the unfathomable mystery of his love part of God's own self-definition.[13]

In creation God determines God's own being as interactive; in doing so God actualizes God's own nature as the one who is love in particular, contingent ways.

The relationship of God to the world must be a reciprocal, dialogical one. God cannot be understood as alone significant to the world. The

---

[12] W. Kasper, *Jesus the Christ* (New York: Paulist Press, 1976), p. 95.

[13] J. J. O'Donnell, S. J. *Trinity and Temporality* (Oxford: Oxford University Press, 1983), p. 200.

world and human history are also significant to God. Creation is a work of divine humility. The world is not a matter of indifference to God. While creation is marked by God's own imprint, namely, the image of God, God in a real but different way is marked by the world.

While God transcends history, history is important and makes a difference to God. God is not simply above history—unaffected and unchanged by it. There is therefore a helplessness in God that is corollary to the character of Creation and Incarnation. This helplessness is freely chosen and is not ultimate. Divine omnipotence is defined as the ultimate triumph of God's unchanging will of love. The key word here is *ultimate*. God has freely accepted temporal helplessness in the interest of open personal relation with God's creatures. There is real interdependence and reciprocity between God and the world. This interdependence does not spring from the limitation of God's essential being but from voluntary self-limitation.

Because creation is an act of self-limitation, God in some mysterious way has put himself at a disadvantage; God has let himself be at the mercy of God's own creation. Simone Weil has underlined this paradoxical nature of God's love: "A victim of misfortune is lying in the road, half-dead with hunger. God pities him but cannot send him bread. But I am here and luckily I am not God. I can give him a piece of bread. It is my one point of superiority over God."[14] Divine creativity involves risk; the risk of being denied. The creating God is not, according to H. Küng, "a God of solitude, but a God of partnership, of the covenant. He is not an apathetic, unfeeling, impassible but a sympathetic, compassionate God."[15] God's power resides in its ability to evoke a response while respecting the integrity of the other. In that process it opens itself to refusal and therefore to suffering.

The activity of God in creation must be precarious. It must proceed by no assured program. Each step is a precarious step into the unknown. If creation is the work of love, then its shape cannot be predetermined. God is determined to be God only in relationship to God's creation. That is the risk of God's infinite love. So eternal love can become suffering love because of its openness to be refused. As Moltmann writes:

---

[14]Simone Weil, *First and Last Notebooks*, trans. by R. Rees (London: Oxford University Press, 1970), p. 297.

[15]H. Küng, *On Being a Christian* (Garden City: Doubleday, 1974), p. 30.

God is not **unchangeable** if to be unchangeable means that he could not in the freedom of his love open himself to the changeable history of his creation. God is not **incapable of suffering** if this means that in the freedom of his love he would not be receptive to suffering over the contradiction of man and the self-destruction of his creation. God is **not invulnerable** if this means that he could not open himself to the pain of the cross. God is **not perfect** if this means that he did not in the craving of his love want his creation to be necessary to his perfection.[16]

According to Moltmann, "God takes man so seriously that he suffers under the actions of man."[17] The suffering of love is one in which one voluntarily opens oneself to the possibility of being affected by another. The justifiable denial that God is capable of suffering because of a deficiency in God's being may not lead to a denial that God is incapable of suffering out of the fullness of God's being, i.e., love. Contrary to Greek thought, God suffers not out of imperfection but out of the plenitude of God's love.

Suffering in God does not spring from the limitation of God's essential being but from voluntary self-limitation and self-expression of God's love for others. The suffering of God does not imply the limitation of God's essential nature, but it rather signifies God's strength to limit himself.

---

[16] J. Moltmann, *The Church in the Power of the Spirit* (New York: Harper and Row, 1975), p. 62.

[17] "The more the covenant is taken seriously as the revelation of God, the more profoundly one can understand the historicity of God and history in God. If God has opened his heart in the covenant with his people, he is injured by disobedience and suffers in the people. What the Old Testament terms *the wrath of God* does not belong in the category of the anthropomorphic transference of lower human emotions to God, but in the category of the divine *pathos*. His wrath is injured love and therefore a mode of his reaction to men. Love is the source and the basis of the possibility of the wrath of God. The opposite of love is not wrath, but indifference. Indifference towards justice and injustice would be a retreat on the part of God from the covenant. But his wrath is an expression of his abiding interest in man. Anger and love do not therefore keep a balance. 'His wrath lasts for the twinkling of an eye,' and, as the Jonah story shows, God takes back his anger for the sake of his love in reaction to human repentance. As injured love, the wrath of God is not something that is inflicted, but a divine suffering of evil. It is a sorrow which goes through his opened heart. He suffers in his passion for his people." J. Moltmann, *The Crucified God* (New York: Harper and Row, 1975) pp. 271–272.

To say that God suffers is to say that God is actively engaged in dealing with a history which is real to God. At no point does God overwhelm human freedom. The genuine freedom of the created to do what God has not willed is guaranteed by the self-limitation of God in bringing freedom into being. It is thus that freedom is real, and the future open, that history is history. God acts in the future through our freedom and is limited by our freedom. The future is undecided, open, and so is unknowable in principle even to God. God as the eternal one does not merely establish time by creating it, but freely assumes it as a specification of God's own self. As D. Dawe writes:

> In creation, God accepted the limitation of co-existence with man and the world, which have their own creativity and freedom. Hence as long as there is a real human history in which men are acting freely and as long as God is concerned with men, there is some aspect of the divine being that is only potentially perfect. If God has a relationship with creation, and the created order has some measure of freedom, then there is an element of openness or incompleteness in the divine being.[18]

God's freedom to act is anchored in love and is therefore characterized by unchangeableness. The unchangeable quality in God is God's will to love: God's unswerving faithfulness to God's covenant. God's immutability cannot be understood primarily in a static way. God's immutability is dynamic and historical. It implies the dynamic capacity for infinite responsive change in the interests of God's fixed purpose of love. God has unlimited "ego strength" in his relation to his creation. In his holy "mutability" God has the ability to stay integrated in the fulfillment of his fundamental purpose of love. God's selfhood remains unimpaired no matter how deeply and intimately God becomes involved with creation, with God's people. If anything is immutable in God it is the completeness of God's love for us, which must include responses to our everchanging needs.

The change that is denied to God is a change that rests on the incompletion of the subject, whose potency is not yet fully actualized. If God is God then such a mutability cannot be predicated of God. But does

---

[18] D. Dawe, *The Form of a Servant* (Philadelphia: Fortress Press, 1964), p. 189.

change always involve imperfection, a transition from potency to act? The whole question here consists in the nature of perfection. The problem is how to conceive the perfection of God properly. How can God be understood as the perfect reality and yet open to change and growth? Immutability, changelessness, are static attributes. They may be useful in describing the being of God; they do not provide a useful understanding of God as personal agent, of God in God's relatedness. The Bible pictures God as involved with creation, and creation as a kenotic act of God cannot be understood through static metaphors. Biblical thought is dominated by a highly personal conception of God. This personalism is best characterized by the attribute of freedom given to God. God is not determined by some abstract metaphysical necessity.

God's becoming is not the fulfilling of a need because of which God should be dependent on others, but it is the communication of God's richness by which, in complete freedom, God makes himself dependent on an other. God does not change nor is God changed by God's own fulfillment. But we are saying too little if we make God a mover who always remains unmoved. God changes in the causing of being and becoming of the realities God has created and does so in a fully divine way without compulsion, in freedom and in love. The immutability of God is a dialectical truth like the unity of God. Karl Rahner has attempted to explain this dialectic in the following fashion: although God "is immutable in and of himself, he himself can become something in another."[19] According to Rahner, this possibility is not rooted in an imperfection, "but the height of his perfection. This perfection would be less perfect if he could not become less than he is . . . The absolute, or, more correctly, the absolute One in the pure freedom of his infinite unrelatedness, which he always preserves, possesses the possibility of himself becoming the other, the finite."[20] This possibility is the possibility of kenosis: the other is established as God's own reality through a dispossession of self, through a giving away of self. While in creation this kenosis is not complete, not full, and therefore the other established by God is not fully himself, still creation is the becoming of God in the other. God as personal agent is changed and affected existentially, not

---

[19]K. Rahner, *Foundations of Christian Faith* (New York: Crossroad, 1978), p. 221.
[20]Ibid., p. 222.

structurally, by the constitution of the other. The change is dialogical; God's personal being is enriched or depleted by the character of our relationship with God. God has willed to be God not for himself alone but also for us and this decision affects God's own being.

P. Hodgson writes: "God will not be the same God upon the consummation of all things and their return to the Father as he was prior to the act of creation. In this sense he will have 'become' something 'other' and will have experienced something 'more' than was the case when God was God for himself alone."[21] Creativity at whatever level is affirmation of the Other, a giving of being, a sharing. *Actio fit in passo:* the activity of the agent is *in* the "other," is the "other" as brought into being, an "other" who is a center of action and creativity.

The doctrine of creation "ex nihilo" has often been understood so as to indicate the establishment of an infinite gap between God and man/woman, a gap that could be bridged only by another action of God: by a redemptive incarnation. The danger of this approach to creation is its underlying presupposition that man/woman has his/her roots in nothingness. What creation "out of nothing" means to say is that creation is totally from God and therefore totally and radically dependent upon God. The roots are in God's own "nothingness." Through God's graciousness the creature is no less infinite than the creator, in the infinity of its receptivity: *Homo capax infiniti.* In his/her deepest religious experience, man/woman realizes the coincidence of finitude and infinity, the infinity of his/her finitude. The infinite has shared its own infinite being. To be a creature is to be both finite and a sharer in the infinite.

Our finitude in our creatureliness is the corollary of divine creativity. We participate in that creativity. Paul Tillich wrote:

> The doctrine of creation is not the story of an event which took place 'once upon a time.' It is the basic description of the relation between God and the world. It is the correlate to the analysis of man's finitude. It answers the question implied in man's finitude and in finitude generally. In giving this answer, it discovers that the meaning of finitude is creatureliness.[22]

---

[21] P. Hodgson, *Jesus—Word and Presence, An Essay in Christology* (Philadelphia: Fortress Press, 1971), p. 128.

[22] P. Tillich, *Systematic Theology,* Vol. I, (Chicago: University of Chicago Press, 1951), p. 252.

We cannot view God and man/woman as two beings, competing with each other. The real distinction between God and men/women is in the fact of human finitude. Men/women have their permanent and ongoing origin in God. Created reality and, in a special way, human beings, find their own authentic existence, freedom and autonomy insofar as they live out their dependence upon God. Radical poverty is the very nature of created reality; it is the orientation of created reality to the incomprehensible mystery that God is.

While creation through self-bestowal means that God is immanent to God's creation, and that creation's nature is a for-Godness, it also means that God does not have to intervene from outside of God's creation. The expression "from outside" as applied to God's creating and even to God's revelation is not an adequate one. God never acts in anything really from outside because God is present in everything that exists distant from God, as the deepest foundation of that existence, as Creator. God is not encompassed by what exists distant from God, but is certainly always more deeply present in it than that reality is to itself.

Through creation God establishes reality truly as different from, although always from God. God gives of himself in such a way that what is established is established in its difference from himself. Creation as a self-limiting act on the part of God is the establishment by God of what is other precisely as other.

The dimension of "otherness" is essentially related to an understanding of creation as *ex nihilo*. There is an authentic autonomy of all earthly realities but never in independence of God.

In the same way that there is an order in the universe grounded transcendentally in God, there is also a freedom grounded in the freedom of God. Creativity implies for God respect for the "other." This must also be the case for human creativity. Creativity, at whatever level it is affirmed, is an affirmation of the "other," a giving of being, a sharing. The other is in turn a center of action and creativity. The gift is the giving that is given. What is shared is itself a sharing. It is the "Other" addressing me who alone can shake and call into question my egoism, requiring me to take into account another center of meaning and valuation, another orientation into the world.

Emphasis on creation is emphasis on exteriority, on the decentering of the self; it is emphasis on the "other" (the neighbor). Given the advent of the "other," we know ourselves to be not alone; consequently, we cannot responsibly avoid relationship with the "other." The advent of the "other" reveals that our freedom, insofar as it is related only to itself, is arbitrarily created freedom and is determined by both the physical and the social voluntary. Writing about Genesis 1:26–27, P. Hodgson affirms:

> In the Genesis passage, human freedom is defined in terms of certain constitutive *relationships:* the relationship to God, in whose image we are created; the relation to the earth and its living creatures, over which 'A Dham' is to have dominion; and the relationship between man and woman as the primordial community in which human beings can be free "for the other."[23]

Again, "the essence of the human being is *created, embodied freedom*— a freedom limited by and reciprocal with the body (both individual and collective, organic and social), an incarnate, contingent, finite freedom, yet still a freedom."[24]

As such creatureliness retains a heritage of non-being; *creatio ex nihilo* is also *creatio in nihilo* and consequently a creation that is threatened and only partially protected against such a threat. *Creatio ex* and *in nihilo* implies the precariousness of creation. It implies that God is presented and addressed to us as the one who is absent in the way God only can be absent, but also in a way that permits us to define ourselves in a fashion that would otherwise be impossible.

The possibility of definability is linked to our initial nothingness. As J. P. Sartre wrote: "If man is not definable, it is because to begin with he is nothing. He will not be anything until later, and then he will be what he makes of himself."[25] Nothingness is the space for freedom and creativity. Freedom begins as an act of negation. As Berdyaev wrote: "Freedom is not created by God . . . it is part of the nothing out of which God created the world."[26] As such, freedom can only be known through the exercise of freedom. It is known in the moment of

---

[23] P. Hodgson, *Jesus—Word and Presence*, pp. 123–124.
[24] Ibid. p. 126.
[25] Jean-Paul Sartre, "Existentialism is a Humanism," in *Existentialism from Dostoyevsky to Sartre*, ed. W. Kaufmann, (New York: Harper and Row, 1956), p. 290.
[26] N. Berdyaev, *The Destiny of Man* (New York: Harper and Row, 1960), p. 25.

creativity: bringing about the other as other out of nothing. As Macquarrie writes: "Out of nothing that is not yet determined, they bring forth something to which they have given a definite shape. In doing this, they are themselves experiencing creativity."[27] The fundamental form of freedom is creativity, "the human freedom to shape humanity." The limit of that shaping is our creatureliness.

From the concept of creation "ex nihilo" derives the notion of contingency, in the sense that creation depends on God entirely for its origins and for what it continues to be in its existence and its order. By contingency one understands that creation has no self-subsistence and no ultimate stability of its own. Whatever is, is in relationship to the Creator. The created being is not its own author, does not possess its own starting point, and cannot protect itself against contingency.

Creation at the beginning is the creation of time and it must be understood as *creatio mutabilis*. It is not perfect, but perfectible. It is an open system, not a balanced and fulfilled reality. It is open to the history of both damnation and salvation. Creation as finite, perfectible, and fallible is eminently redeemable. Yet because of its tendency to an open and infinite horizon, human existence can never be ultimately and finally satisfied with its own power, or self. Nor can it be redeemed by itself. The language of humanism which understands liberation to be a goal attainable by human effort must give place to a language of faith. The language of faith, in Paul Lehmann's words, "insist(s) that the achievement of humanization comes by the reality and power of a deliverance which occurs in history from beyond history and refuses to abandon history."[28] As Ernest Bloch affirmed, "It takes total 'Otherness' to give the appropriate measure of depth to everything that has been longed for in deifying man."[29] Freedom that yearns to be radical freedom is in need of a liberation from beyond, which is also from within.

A Christology that can address some of the most difficult problems encountered in the question of Christian ethics must be understood from the creation-perspective outlined above.

---

[27] J. Macquarrie, *In Search of Humanity* (New York: Crossroad, 1983), p. 14.

[28] P. Lehmann, *Ideology and Incarnation* (Geneva: John Knox Association, 1962), p. 26.

[29] Ernst Bloch, *Man On His Own,* trans. E. B. Ashton (New York: Herder and Herder, 1970), pp. 154–155.

The whole development of Christology from Chalcedon up to our own time has been dominated by the "God-man" formula: Jesus Christ is "truly God" and "truly man." All the formulas that have emerged in the course of this history have been intended as logical explanations of this union.

The core and crucial question of the whole Christological tradition is the question of the living unity of God and man in Jesus Christ, with the continuing differentiation of the two: the personal unity of God and man in Jesus Christ. The unity of God and man in Jesus Christ has been classically expressed in the doctrine of the hypostatic unity. The hypostatic unity means that God is so radically present to Jesus' own subjectivity that Jesus' own identity is God-given and yet his own. The hypostatic union is the affirmation that while God and man are radically different yet they are one in Jesus Christ.

While the whole theological tradition sees the unity of Jesus as hypostatic in and with the eternal Logos, the Second Person of the Trinity, the New Testament sees the unity of Jesus primarily as that of Jesus in the Father. According to the New Testament, Jesus' human consciousness is turned not to the Logos but to the Father. Jesus knows himself to be one with the Father, not with a divine hypostasis differentiated from him. Jesus' unity with the Father is expressed in his behavior towards the Father, one of obedience and total dedication to the point of self-sacrifice. Jesus relates to the Father as a free subject to a free subject. According to Karl Rahner, " . . . the human nature of Christ as the person of the Logos must be understood in such a way that Christ in reality and in all truth is a man with all that involves: a human consciousness which is aware in adoration of its own infinite distance in relation to God; a spontaneous human interior life and freedom with a history which because it is that of God himself, possesses not less but more independence, for the latter is not diminished but increased by union with God."[30]

Jesus stands before God in free human obedience. He is Mediator, according to K. Rahner, "not only in virtue of the ontological union of two natures, but also through his (Jesus') activity, which is directed to

---

[30] K. Rahner, "Incarnation," in *Encyclopedia of Theology. The Concise Sacramentum Mundi.* (New York: The Seabury Press, 1975), p. 695.

God (as obedience to the will of the Father) and cannot be conceived of simply as God's activity in and through a human nature thought of as purely instrumental, a nature which in relation to the Logos would be ontologically and morally, purely passive."[31] The unity of Jesus with God can be found only in the historical existence of Jesus in his message and actions. The starting point for the question of the hypostatic unity is the history and destiny of Jesus of Nazareth, his relation to the Father in dedication and obedience.

What is revealed in Jesus is the right relationship between man/woman and God and God's relationship to creation. In the person of Jesus we have a model of the right interaction of human and divine creativity of the reciprocity of divine and human freedom. Creation and Incarnation are not two different modes of God's causal relationship to us.

The mystery of the Incarnation understood in light of our theology of creation implies that when God gives of himself, even fully, God does not do violence to the other, but gives it full authenticity. Jesus is the one who sees himself and the whole of his life in the context of receiving and giving. Receiving is the fundamental expression of his being. In self-surrender, in self-emptying, in accepting to be fulfilled by God, Jesus posits his own existence. This is actualized by letting-go. In Jesus we have the affirmation that the more deeply one is accepted by God and is taken into God's own existence, the more one discovers oneself, the more radically one is made free for one's own possibilities. Being accepted and independence are not opposed, but rather they correspond to one another. Jesus of Nazareth is the one who, from the very depths of his being, has surrendered himself to God and has been accepted by God. Jesus lived his life in complete dependence on his Father.[32] But such dependence does not destroy human personality. One is never so truly and fully personal as when one is living in complete dependence on God. This is how a human personality comes into its own. This is not impersonal humanity, but humanity at its most personal.

Because receiving is Jesus' fundamental nature, his life is lived out

---

[31] K. Rahner, "Current Problems in Christology," in *Theological Investigations*, Vol. I (Baltimore: Helicon, 1965), p. 161.

[32] K. Rahner, "Theological Observations on the Concept of Time," *Theological Investigations*, Vol. XI (New York: The Seabury Press, 1974), p. 290.

in giving, in a pouring out of self, and ultimately in a complete giving, his dying on the cross. Jesus' answer to God's self-emptying love is in his own self-emptying. By emptying himself Jesus participated fully in the life of God, the plenitude of being. Self-emptying, the principle of the kenotic Being of God, became the law of Jesus' own life. Jesus universalized this law: "Whoever would save his life shall lose it, and whoever loses his life for my sake and the gospel will save it" (Mk 8:35; John 12:24). All personal reality must go out of itself in order to preserve itself. The "I" must empty itself at a "Thou" in order to gain itself in the other. Whatever exists finds its identity not through an absolute, aloof being-in-itself, but concretely, and only through a relationship. Jesus does not find his nature in being, an hypostasis, a self-substance, which has always been regarded as the highest perfection; instead it is his nature to exist for others, it is self-surrender, self-abandonment; he is the one who steps aside, who stands up for others and identifies with others. Jesus' personhood possesses both passive and active qualities. On the one hand, and this is primary, it contains the element of surrender or self-negation, in relation to the Father; on the other hand it invites a dedication to the neighbor. The thou of the Father and the thou of the neighbor are constitutive of Jesus' own personhood. The depth of Jesus' personhood is measured in terms of his relation to God and to neighbor. These relations determine the concrete essence of his person. Jesus' "ego" comes not from himself, but from beyond himself, from the Father and from the neighbor. To be constituted by these singular relationships is to be unconditionally responsive. In being fully responsive to the Father and to the oppressed, Jesus is the Son of God. Jesus' divine sonship is his humanness to the utmost.

What we have in the person of Jesus as the Christ is intensified creation. In Jesus Christ the dimension of creatureliness is not eliminated but sharpened. As J. B. Metz writes: "The human nature of Christ is not 'lessened' by being taken up into the divine Logos, made simply into a dead tool, a mere accessory, a gesture of God within the world, but given its hitherto unsuspected full human authenticity: Jesus Christ was fully man, indeed more human than any of us."[33] Being "accepted" by God

---

[33] J. B. Metz, *Theology of the World*, trans. W. Glen-Doepel (New York: Herder and Herder, 1969), p. 26.

is a freeing act since it is fundamentally a kenotic act. Again, Metz writes: "God's divinity consists in the fact that he does not remove the difference between himself and what is other, but rather accepts the other precisely as different from himself."[34] To be accepted by God is to be set free to be oneself. In Jesus we have the unique culmination of the general creator-creation relationship. In his personal unity with God, Jesus is the fulfillment of the human destiny.

Jesus' unity with God is the fulfillment of the openness to God that is constitutive of human reality as such. According to Rahner, " . . . the Incarnation of God is the unique and highest instance of the actualization of the essence of human reality which consists in this: that man is insofar as he abandons himself to the absolute mystery whom we call God. Anyone who understands correctly what an obediential potency for the hypostatic union means, and what it really means to say human nature can be assumed by the person as the Word of God, . . . knows that the obediential potency cannot be an individual potency alongside other potencies in the structure of human beings, but rather is objectively identical with man's essence."[35]

Human destiny is to have its origin permanently in God, to be permanently grounded in absolute mystery; to be radically different and yet one with God. Being from God and being totally dependent upon God in no way cancels out human personhood, individuality or independence. The deepest self of man/woman is constituted by its relationship with God. This is directly related to man/woman's capacity for the infinite. The actualization of that capacity through God's graciousness constitutes the deepest dimension of a person's self-being. God's transcendence consists in the fact that God does not remove the difference between himself and what is other, but rather accepts the other precisely as different from himself. The more a creature participates in God's being, the more the creature is someone itself. To think of God or the creature as threatening the other is to fail to think of "in itselfness" and "for-the-otherness" as mutually fostering, mutually inclusive. In other words it is a failure to think dialogically.

The basic question to be dealt with in the area of the specificity of

---

[34] Ibid.
[35] K. Rahner, *Foundations of Christian Faith,* op. cit., p. 218.

Christian ethics as was previously affirmed is Christianity's claim to a universal vocation founded in its belief in the absoluteness of its savior, Jesus Christ, as the indispensable mediator of salvation. In fact Christianity defines humanhood and Godhood in terms of Jesus Christ.

In the context of an historically conditioned revelation there is evidently a great problem in affirming that a particular human life is the absolute and definitive norm in history. As Rigali writes:

> Since history is the essence of a human life, to designate a human life as the absolute, definitive norm of the *humanum* in history is to say, paradoxically, that this human life, this historical reality *as such,* transcends all historical reality as its norm or ideal.
>
> We should emphasize the paradox here. It is not paradox but mystery that Christ *as divine* transcends history or that his grace is offered universally to all persons. It is a paradox, however, that Jesus Christ *as human,* as the particular *historical reality* that his human life is, transcends history as its norm. More sharply stated, the paradox is that Jesus Christ *precisely as historical, precisely as humanum,* transcends the *humanum* of history-in-progress; as *humanum,* he is "the concrete universal."[36]

That the humanity of Jesus has universal significance means that in some real way it has a determinative effect on all persons in their relation to what is considered as ultimate in their lives. Schillebeeckx poses the problem in the following way:

> The problem now confronting us is: Can such a unique universality be present and be recognized in one historical person, Jesus of Nazareth? To put it another way: Does this man, Jesus of Nazareth, confessed by his followers at the time as the Christ, Son of God and Lord, still have importance for us today, in such manner that we too can find in him definitive and conclusive salvation? The underlying problem is bound up with the question of how a particular event in history can have a universal significance for all human beings, and therefore

---

[36]Norbert Rigali, S. J. "Christ and Morality," in *Readings in Moral Theology No. 2: The Distinctiveness of Christian Ethics,* op. cit., p. 115.

for us now. If this is even possible, it would seem to require a historical intermediary.[37]

To posit the mystery of the Incarnation within the broader mystery of Creation is to establish the proper grounds for the absoluteness and universality of Jesus Christ as savior and to assign proper limits to Christianity's claims. Emphasis on the insertion of the order of Redemption within the order of Creation leads to an emphasis on the historicity and unfinishedness of the Incarnation. The claim about the unique and universal significance of Jesus cannot bypass history. In a variety of ways it has to be tested empirically.

In a real sense, who Jesus is can only be understood from his historical existence; and since one's identity is ultimately meaningful in proportion to one's capacity to make history, who Jesus is can only be understood from studying the difference he has made, is making and can make to others and to the world. In this historical context, Jesus is called Lord because he has shown himself to be compassionate and has affected our lives. As Hellwig writes, "we call Jesus divine Lord and Savior-Christ on historical, relational grounds, because of the import he had and because of the way human structures and systems shape themselves in response to him."[38] To assert the uniqueness of Jesus the Christ, is not to assert that he alone is constitutive of history as salvific, but that in relation to him and in interdependence with him, we also can contribute and share. As Warren Groff writes:

> Faith has no timeless platform that lifts it outside the vulnerability of the historical realm. It boasts no certainty other than what accrues to a contingent event from the past, with its promise of claiming the present in the name of a purposive future. The person-event of Christ precedes particular responses of faith. Yet it is precisely by means of such responses—those of the original witness no less than their successors—that revelation has its on-going content and power, so completely is the truth of faith tied in with what is transmitted historically.

---

[37]Schillebeeckx, *Jesus, op. cit.*, p. 603.
[38]Monika Hellwig, "Christology and Attitudes Toward Social Structures," in *Above Every Name*, Thomas Clarke, ed. (New York: Paulist Press, 1980), p. 23.

> Christological language is meaningful in relation to the actual life and impact of the man Jesus. And this relationship is made accessible to the present generation through the contribution of those who have already responded to that alteration of social-personal existence which roots in this Jesus.[39]

In some real way Christ's universality rests on discipleship, on the disciples' faithfulness to the demands of the Kingdom. Whatever humanness is revealed to us in Jesus Christ cannot be seen as having been blueprinted in heaven but "is intensely and creatively his own [and so] is able to mediate the divine silence that is wholly other than it. What makes us recognize him as Lord is not that we are able to look at a divine model with whom to compare him, but rather that we are able to experience the integrating, healing force of his presence in the interrelationships of human freedom."[40] We recognize him as Lord because of a human struggle that involves creative and constitutive decision-making by Jesus and others aligned with him, including contemporary believers. To deal historically with the person of Jesus as revelation is to have to think eschatologically. The universality of Jesus Christ is not preexistent and already given, but is rather an eschatological expectation. Process and development of humanhood is essential. As John Macquarrie writes:

> The Christian, we have seen, defines mature manhood in terms of Jesus Christ, and especially his self-giving love. But Christ himself is not a static figure, nor are Christians called to imitate him as a static model. Christ is the eschatological figure, always before us; and the doctrine of his coming again "with glory" implies that there are dimensions of christhood not manifest in the historical Jesus and not yet fully grasped by the disciples. Thus discipleship does not restrict human development to some fixed pattern, but summons into freedom, the full depth of which is unknown, except that it will always be consonant with self-giving love.[41]

---

[39]Warren Groff, *Christ the Hope of the Future* (Grand Rapids, Mich., Eerdmans, 1971), p. 47.

[40]Monika Hellwig, art. cit. p. 27.

[41]John Macquarrie, *Principles of Christian Theology* (New York: Scribner Sons, 1966), p. 249.

The order of Redemption is not a counterculture; it does not create an alternative realm to the created one; salvation is not against, not above, not separate from the order of creation. While the two orders are not identical they are not historically distinguishable. There is oneness without identity; this implies that ontologically both orders are grounded in the same divine reality. "Creation, reconciliation and consummation are not separate acts but only distinguishable aspects of one awe-inspiring movement of God—his love or letting-be, whereby he confers, sustains, and perfects the being of the creatures."[42]

In the realm of ethics, the acknowledgment of the basic continuity of Creation-Redemption has important consequences: the precariousness, historicity and contingency of all beings. Nature and the world have to be experienced as that which is not-God. Yet finitude is not to be considered a flaw. God's salvation can never result in the removal of human finitude. Contingency is not abrogated by Redemption; it remains as the essential characteristic of human existence in the world. There is nothing about creation and the new creation that is in itself un-historical, non-contingent; everything is the interplay or chance and necessity of opportunity and novelty.

The acceptance of contingency and finitude and historicity implies that the newness of the new creation is more of the same original newness. In the context of a conditional and finite humankind, the Paschal Mystery does not add a new super-human level, but rather shows how the essential demands of humanity are to be attained by finite man/woman.

There is but one divine-human history in which the saving power of God is at work. This can be symbolized in the person of Jesus Christ understood as the fulfillment of creation. In Jesus Christ we have the symbol of God's presence to creation and of creation's authentic response.[43]

---

[42]Ibid., p. 247.

[43]As Schillebeeckx writes: "In the New Testament, the story of Jesus is experienced as the illuminating and transforming symbol which discloses to our understanding the depth-dimension of our finite existence. What was expressed in Jesus' words and deeds, his life and death, is evocative for our own human experiences: it discloses our own existence to us; it illuminates what authentic human life can be when we are aware that we are safe in the hands of the living God and can accept it as a challenge. . . . People come

Again, according to E. Schillebeeckx, "The experience of creation, a historically variable experience of fortuitousness and contingency, seems to me to be the permanent breeding ground for any experience of the saving nearness of God, and also for example the special experience that is to be found in Jesus and in the liturgy."[44] Creation and humanhood are the constitutive symbols for us of the real presence of God. Creation is the gateway to the recognition of Jesus as an embodiment and manifestation of God.[45]

To emphasize creation and creaturehood as the basic framework for the specificity of Christian ethics, is to emphasize and to perceive Christian ethics within the paradigm of dialogical communication. The paradigm of dialogical communication grounds the basic sense of common membership and participation in the social world that is necessary for morality itself. The paradigm of dialogue also gives us our necessary sense of identity and place in the on-going historical search for truth and right. Dialogue frames a context for interpreting the basic symbols, myths, metaphors and stories of our Christian tradition.

To image God in and through the person of Jesus Christ understood as intensified creation, is to hold out the more religiously evocative ideal for the creature's emulation as it is concerned with goodness and with a relational kind of power. It is to emphasize that the goodness of God is a receptive relationality that embodies sensitivity and compassion, vulnerability and strength, dependence and responsibility. It is to respond to God's invitation to be as compassionate as God is compas-

---

to know themselves (again) in Jesus the Lord. At the same time, the transforming power of this representative symbol calls us to a conversion in faith; in other words, this correlation is achieved in *metanoia* or conversion, and not in simple alignment." E. Schillebeeckx, *Interim Report* (New York: Crossroad, 1981), p. 60.

[44] E. Schillebeeckx, *Christ: The Experience of Jesus as Lord*, (New York: The Seabury Press, 1980), p. 810.

[45] According to Schillebeeckx: "Creation is a blank cheque for which God himself stands guarantor. It is a vote of confidence which gives the person who believes in the Creator God courage to believe, in word and action, that despite many experiences of disaster, the kingdom of God, i.e. human salvation and happiness, is in fact in the making for mankind, in the power of God's creation which summons human beings to its realization." E. Schillebeeckx, *God Among Us: The Gospel Proclaimed* (New York: Crossroad, 1983), p. 104.

sionate; i.e., to relate creatively to the world, not by exercising dominion, but by participation in the process of continuing creation.

Jesus' own dialogical relationship to God is for the Christian the paradigm of our dialogue with God and others that makes our own religious and moral lives possible. The Christian imagery of grace and love, where persons become intimate, though not identified, leads to a certain understanding of our "equality" with God. Being created in the image of God, human beings become as it were "equal" partners with God in the furthering of creation's goals. Both partners in this exchange are speakers and listeners; both are needful of the other. The successful completion of the project of Creation is precarious; the dialogue is therefore a practical one: a task of building societal structures, institutions and policies that lead to authentic humanhood.

At a time of moral disarray, various segments of the population in the United States are seeking to rebuild structures of values. The task of discerning what are the basic Christian ethical values to the American cannot be more timely; the task of correlating these specific values to the American cultural context is imperative. While a consensus on profound ethical problems within a pluralistic society may never be arrived at, Christianity needs to be a participant in the contemporary debate. While respecting the private conscience of individuals the necessity of such a participation is intrinsic to Christianity itself. For Christianity claims for itself a culturally redemptive presence. We read in *Gaudium et Spes*

> The good news of Christ continually renews the life and culture of fallen man; it combats and removes the error and evil which flow from the ever-present attraction of sin. It never ceases to purify and elevate the morality of peoples. It takes the spiritual qualities and endowments of every age and nation, and with supernatural riches it causes them to blossom, as it were, from within; it fortifies, completes and restores them in Christ. In this way the Church carries out its mission and in that very act it stimulates and advances human and civil culture, as well as contributing by its activity, including liturgical activity, to a man's interior freedom.[46]

---

[46]*Gaudium et Spes*, No. 58, p. 963.

In *Evangelii Nuntiandi* (1976), Paul VI made it clear that evangelization is not limited to preaching or to ministries of the literal word. In words that appear surprisingly radical, he identifies the scope of evangelization with the transformation of the human realm: "It is a question not only of preaching the Gospel in ever wider geographic areas or to ever greater numbers of people, but also of affecting and as it were upsetting, through the power of the Gospel, mankind's criteria of judgment, determining values, points of interest, lines of thought, sources of inspiration, and models of life, which are in contrast with the word of God and the plan of salvation."[47] Evangelization will clearly have a counter-cultural thrust for, as Paul VI affirms, "what matters is to evangelize human culture and cultures, not in a purely decorative way as it were by applying a thin veneer, but in a vital way, in depth, and right to their very roots."[48] This counter-cultural thrust of evangelization is not without difficulties and yet "the split between the Gospel and culture is without a doubt the drama of our time . . . every effort must be made to ensure a full evangelization of culture, or more correctly, of cultures. They have to be regenerated by an encounter with the Gospel."[49]

Christianity's transformative insertion into cultures is compared at Vatican II to the mystery of the Incarnation in which the Divine Logos accommodated itself to human reality.

> In his self-revelation to his people culminating in the fullness of manifestation in his incarnate Son, God spoke according to the culture proper to each age. Similarly the Church has existed through the centuries in varying circumstances and has utilized the resources of different cultures in its preaching to spread and explain the message of Christ, to examine and understand it more deeply, and to express it more perfectly in the liturgy and in various aspects of the life of the faithful.[50]

The distinctiveness of Christian ethics can only be the consequence of an ongoing Incarnation. As such it will clearly be historical and open-ended. "It is not yet clear what we are to become."

---

[47]"Evangelization in the Modern World" (Washington: USCC. 1976), No. 19, p. 16.
[48]Ibid.
[49]Ibid., p. 17.
[50]*Gaudium et Spes,* No. 58, p. 962; Cf. also *Ad Gentes,* No. 10, p. 824–25.

Bibliography

Faith and Ethics

Baelz, P. R. *Ethics and Belief* (London: Sheldon Press, 1977).

Crossin, John W. *What Are They Saying About Virtue?* (New Jersey: Paulist Press, 1985).

D'Arcy, Eric. *Human Acts: An Essay in Their Moral Evaluation* (London: Oxford University Press, 1963).

Edwards, George. *Jesus and the Politics of Violence* (New York: Harper and Row, 1972).

Evans, Donald. *Struggle and Fulfillment: The Inner Dynamics of Religion and Morality* (Philadelphia: Fortress Press, 1981).

Gallagher, John, C.S.P. *The Basis for Christian Ethics* (New Jersey: Paulist Press, 1985).

Green, M. *Religious Reason: The Rational and Moral Basis of Religious Belief* (New York: Oxford University Press, 1978).

Gula, Richard M., S.S. *What Are They Saying About Moral Norms?* (New York: Paulist Press, 1982).

Hanigan, James P. *As I Have Loved You: The Challenge of Christian Ethics* (New Jersey: Paulist Press, 1986).

Harrod, Howard L. *The Human Center: Moral Agency in the Social World* (Philadelphia: Fortress Press, 1981).

Little, David and Twiss, Sumner B. *Comparative Religious Ethics: A New Method* (San Francisco: Harper & Row, 1978).

McClendon, James Wm., Jr. and Smith, James M. *Understanding Religious Convictions* (Notre Dame: University of Notre Dame Press, 1975).

McDonagh, Enda. *Gift and Call* (St. Meinrad: Abbey Press, 1975).

MacIntyre, Alasdair. *After Virtue: A Study in Moral Theology* (Notre Dame: University of Notre Dame Press, 1981).

MacIntyre, Alasdair. *Secularization and Moral Change* (London: Oxford University Press, 1967).

MacNamara, J. V. *Faith and Ethics* (Dublin: Gill & Macmillan, 1985).

MacQuarrie, J. *Three Issues in Ethics* (New York: Harper and Row, 1970).

Meilaender, Gilbert C. *The Theory and Practice of Virtue* (Notre Dame: University of Notre Dame Press, 1984).

Mitchell, B. G. *Morality: Religious and Secular* (Oxford: The Clarendon Press, 1980).

Niebuhr, H. Richard. *The Responsible Self* (New York: Harper and Row, 1963).

New Testament and Ethics

Barr, Sydney O. *The Christian New Morality: A Biblical Study of Situation Ethics* (New York: Oxford University Press, 1969).

Bartlett, David. *The Shape of Biblical Authority* (Philadelphia: Fortress Press, 1983).

Birch, Bruce C. and Rasmussen, Larry L. *Bible and Ethics in the Christian Life* (Minneapolis: Augsburg Publishing Co., 1976).

Curran, Charles and McCormick, Richard, eds. *The Use of Scripture in Moral Theology. Readings in Moral Theology No. 4* (New York: Paulist Press, 1984).

Deidun, Thomas J. *New Covenant Morality in Paul* (Rome: Biblical Institute Press, 1981).

Furnish, Victor Paul. *The Love Command in the New Testament* (Nashville: Abingdon Press, 1972).

Furnish, Victor Paul. *The Moral Teachings of Paul* (Nashville: Abingdon, 1979).

Furnish, Victor Paul. *Theology and Ethics in Paul* (Nashville: Abingdon, 1968).

Garden, Clinton, E. *Biblical Faith and Social Ethics* (New York: Harper, 1960).

Gerhardsson, Birger. *The Ethos of The Bible,* trans. Stephen Westerholm (Philadelphia: Fortress Press, 1981).

Harrelson, Walter. *The Ten Commandments and Human Rights* (Philadelphia: Fortress Press, 1980).

Houlden, J.L. *Ethics and the New Testament* (Baltimore: Penguin Books, 1973).

Kimpel, Benjamin Franklin. *Moral Principles in the Bible: A Study of the Contribution of the Bible to a Moral Philosophy* (New York: Philosophical Library, 1956).

Knox, John. *The Ethics of Jesus in the Teaching of the Church* (Nashville: Abingdon Press, 1961).

Kraemer, Hendrik. *The Bible and Social Ethics* (Philadelphia: Fortress Press, 1965).

Manson. T.W. *Ethics and the Gospel* (New York: Charles Scribner's Sons, 1960).

Minear, Paul S. *Commands of Christ: Authority and Implications* (Nashville: Abingdon Press, 1972).

Miranda, Jose P. *Marx and the Bible,* trans. John Eagleson (Maryknoll: Orbis Books, 1974).

Mott, Stephen Charles. *Biblical Ethics and Social Change* (New York: Oxford University Press, 1982)

Muilenburg, James. *The Way of Israel: Biblical Faith and Ethics* (New York: Harper and Row, 1961).

Ogletree, Thomas. *The Use of the Bible in Christian Ethics* (Philadelphia: Fortress Press, 1983).

Perkins, Pheme. *Love Commands in the New Testament* (New York: Paulist Press, 1982).

Sampley, Paul. *Pauline Partnership in Christ: Christian Community and Commitment in Light of Roman Law* (Philadelphia: Fortress Press, 1980).

Sanders, Jack T. *Ethics in the New Testament: Change and Development* (Philadelphia: Fortress Press, 1975).

Schnackenburg, Rudolf. *The Moral Teaching of the New Testament,* trans. J. Holland-Smith and W. J. O'Hara (New York: Herder and Herder, 1965).

Stott, J.R.W. *Christian Counter-Culture. The Message of the Sermon on the Mount* (Leicester, UK: Inter-Varsity, 1978).

White, R.E.O. *Biblical Ethics* (Atlanta: John Knox Press, 1979).

Specific Christian Ethics

Barth, Karl. *Ethics,* trans. G.W. Bromiley (New York: Seabury Press, 1981).

Beach, W. and Niebuhr, H.R. *Christian Ethics: Sources of the Living Tradition* (New York: Ronald Press, 1955).

Brunner, Emil. *The Divine Imperative: A Study in Christian Ethics* (Philadelphia: Westminster, 1947).

Brunner, Emil. *Justice and the Social Order* (New York: Harper, 1945).

Compagnoni, Francesco. *La specificita della morale cristiana* (Bologna: Edizioni Dehoniane, 1972).

Curran, Charles and McCormick, Richard, eds. *The Distinctiveness of Christian Ethics. Readings in Moral Theology No. 2* (New York: Paulist Press, 1980).

Gustafson, James. *Can Ethics Be Christian?* (Chicago: University of Chicago Press, 1975).

Gustafson, James. *Christ and the Moral Life* (New York: Harper and Row, 1968).

Gustafson, James. *Christian Ethics and the Community* (Philadelphia: Pilgrim Press, 1965).

Gustafson, James. *Protestant and Roman Catholic Ethics* (Chicago: University of Chicago Press, 1978).

Hauerwas, Stanley. *A Community of Character: Toward a Constructive Christian Social Ethic* (Notre Dame and London: University of Notre Dame Press, 1981).

Hauerwas, Stanley. *Truthfulness and Tragedy: Further Investigations in Christian Ethics* (Notre Dame: University of Notre Dame Press, 1977).

Henry, Carl F. H. *Christian Personal Ethics* (Grand Rapids: Wm. B. Eerdmans, 1957).

Knudson, A.C. *The Principles of Christian Ethics* (New York: Abingdon, 1943).

Lehmann, Paul. *Ethics in a Christian Context* (New York: Harper and Row, 1963).

Long, Edward LeRoy, Jr. *A Survey of Christian Ethics* (New York, London, Toronto: Oxford University Press, 1967).

Long, Edward LeRoy, Jr. *A Survey of Recent Christian Ethics* (New York, Oxford: Oxford University Press, 1982).

Marck, W. H. M. van der. *Toward a Christian Ethic: A Renewal in Moral Theology,* trans. Denis J. Barrett (Westminster: Newman Press, 1967).

Niebuhr, Reinhold. *An Interpretation of Christian Ethics* (New York: Harper, 1935).

Osborn, Andrew R. *Christian Ethics* (London: Oxford University Press, 1940).

Osborn, Eric. *Ethical Patterns in Early Christian Thought* (New York and Cambridge: Cambridge University Press, 1976).

Outka, Gene H. and Ramsey, Paul, eds. *Norm and Context in Christian Ethics* (New York: Charles Scribner's Sons, 1968).

Ramsey, Paul. *Basic Christian Ethics* (New York: Scribner's, 1950).

Ramsey, Paul. *Christian Ethics and the Sit-in* (New York: Association Press, 1961).

Rasmussen, Albert Terrill. *Christian Ethics: Exerting Christian Influence* (Englewood Cliffs: Prentice-Hall, 1956).

Sittler, Joseph. *The Structure of Christian Ethics* (Baton Rouge: Louisiana State University Press, 1958).

Thomas, George. *Christian Ethics and Moral Philosophy* (New York: Scribner's, 1955).

Thompson, Kenneth. *Christian Ethics and the Dilemmas of Foreign Policy* (Durham: Duke University Press, 1959).

Ward, K. *Ethics and Christianity* (London: Allen and Unwin, 1970).

Wilder, Amos N. *Kerygma, Eschatology, and Social Ethics* (Philadelphia: Fortress Press, 1966).

Winter, Gibson. *Liberating Creation: Foundations of Religious and Social Ethics* (New York: Crossroad Publishing Company, 1981).

Yoder, John Howard. *The Politics of Jesus* (Grand Rapids: Eerdmans, 1972).

Christian Ethics and Natural Law

Battaglia, Anthony. *Toward a Reformulation of Natural Law* (New York: Seabury Press, 1981).

Brown, O.J. *Natural Rectitude and Divine Law in Aquinas* (Toronto: P.I.M.S., 1981).

Curran, Charles E. *Themes in Fundamental Moral Theology* (Notre Dame: University of Notre Dame Press, 1977).

D'Entreves, Alessandro Passerin. *Natural Law: An Introduction to Legal Philosophy* (London: Hutchinson's University Library, 1951).

Fuchs, Josef. *Natural Law: A Theological Investigation*, trans. Helmut Reckter and John A. Dowling (New York: Sheed & Ward, 1965).

Fuchs, Josef. *Personal Responsibility and Christian Morality* (Washington, D.C.: Georgetown University Press, 1983).

Fuller, Lon L. *The Morality of Law* (New Haven: Yale University Press, 1964).

McDonagh, E. "The Law of Christ and Natural Law," ed. G. Dunstan, *Duty and Discernment* (London: S.C.M. Press, 1975).

O'Connell, Timothy E. *Principles for a Catholic Morality* (New York: Seabury, 1978).

Rhyne, C.T. *Faith Establishes the Law*, SBL Dissertation Series 55 (Chico: Scholars Press, 1981).

Christian Ethics and Community

Arrow, Kenneth J. *Social Choice and Individual Values*, 2nd ed. (New York: John Wiley and Sons, 1963).

Geertz, Clifford. *The Interpretation of Cultures* (New York: Harper-Basic Books, 1973).

Habermas, Jurgen. *Communication and the Evolution of Society*, trans. Thomas McCarthy (Boston: Beacon Press, 1976).

Nelson, J. Robert. *The Realm of Redemption* (London: The Epworth Press, 1951).

Ramsey, Paul. *Who Speaks for the Church?* (Nashville: Abingdon Press, 1967).

Wilson, Jackson R. *In Quest of Community* (New York: Oxford University Press, 1970).

Index

Subject

A
analogia: 33
anonymous: 26, 31, 42
anthropocentrism: 47
anthropological: 11, 31, 54, 81
anthropology: 1, 3, 14, 17, 19, 23, 26, 28, 64, 65, 98
authority: 3, 13, 29, 30, 33, 37, 42, 46, 50, 53, 56, 59, 67, 68, 80, 87
autonomous: 8, 9, 10, 11, 16, 22, 39, 70
autonomy: 7, 9, 15, 16, 25, 33, 109

B
baptism: 73
beatitude: 15
Bible: 33, 34, 39, 48, 82, 107
biblical: 12, 27, 31, 41, 44, 45, 46, 52, 57, 59, 60, 107
bipolarity: 94, 95

C
canon: 8, 82
canonicity: 12, 26, 82
categorical: 11, 12, 21, 22, 64, 65, 66
Catholic: 5, 7, 8, 10, 12, 19, 23, 25, 27, 29, 36, 37, 51, 52, 53, 54, 55, 56, 57, 61, 65, 66, 67, 68, 88, 91
Chalcedon: 112

Christ: 4, 5, 10, 11, 19, 20, 21, 22, 23, 24, 25, 26, 27, 28, 29, 30, 31, 32, 33, 34, 35, 37, 38, 41, 42, 43, 44, 45, 46, 47, 48, 49, 50, 52, 54, 55, 56, 57, 59, 62, 63, 64, 65, 66, 69, 71, 72, 75, 80, 81, 86, 87, 89, 90, 93, 94, 95, 96, 97, 98, 103, 112, 114, 116, 117, 118, 119, 120, 121, 122
Christhood: 64, 118
Christian: 1, 2, 3, 5, 7, 8, 10, 11, 12, 14, 19, 20, 21, 22, 23, 24, 25, 26, 28, 29, 30, 31, 32, 34, 35, 36, 37, 38, 39, 41, 42, 43, 44, 45, 46, 47, 48, 49, 50, 51, 52, 53, 54, 55, 56, 57, 58, 62, 63, 64, 65, 66, 67, 68, 71, 72, 73, 75, 76, 77, 78, 79, 80, 82, 83, 85, 86, 87, 88, 89, 91, 92, 93, 94, 95, 96, 97, 98, 99, 100, 103, 111, 116, 118, 120, 121, 122
Christocentric: 3, 4, 5, 23, 44, 48, 54
Christocentrism: 3, 4, 29, 30, 32, 46, 47
Christofascism: 5
Christological: 10, 11, 12, 22, 26, 31, 32, 51, 52, 55, 60, 65, 94, 98, 112, 118
Christologies: 5, 31
Christology: 1, 3, 5, 11, 14, 19, 46, 47, 57, 60, 61, 65, 95, 96, 98, 111, 112
Christomonism: 4
Church: 7, 21, 23, 26, 32, 33, 34, 39, 40, 56, 57, 58, 59, 60, 61, 62, 63, 64, 65, 67, 69, 71, 72, 75, 79, 82, 91, 96, 97, 121, 122
commandments: 13, 21, 32, 35
contextual: 66, 76, 98
contrapletal: 95
corporate: 35, 70, 79
correlate: 29, 108, 121
correlation: 80, 81
cosmology: 46
counter-cultural: 122
covenant: 104, 106
creation: 4, 7, 10, 11, 15, 16, 21, 24, 25, 26, 35, 36, 41, 47, 51, 63, 95, 96, 98, 99, 100, 101, 102, 103, 104, 105, 106, 107, 108, 109, 110, 111, 113, 114, 115, 117, 119, 120, 121
Creator: 13, 16, 33, 36, 55, 98, 99, 102, 103, 108, 109, 111, 115
culture: 1, 2, 36, 38, 40, 69, 70, 73, 121, 122
cultures: 81, 87, 90, 122

D

decalogue: 30
dialectical: 26, 34, 58, 71, 81, 95, 107
dialogical: 91, 103, 108, 115, 120, 121
Dignitatis Humanae: 90
discipleship: 20, 21, 28, 50, 89, 118
doctrine: 26, 32, 47, 56, 59, 60, 69, 95, 96, 98, 100, 108, 112, 118
doctrines: 85, 95, 96

E

election: 32, 42
elective: 89
evangelical: 24, 79
evolution: 63, 71
existence: 8, 9, 11, 15, 17, 18, 22, 23, 24, 25, 26, 35, 38, 45, 63, 64, 65, 66, 68, 71, 72, 73, 76, 77, 80, 82, 86, 91, 92, 94, 102, 103, 109, 111, 113, 117, 118, 119
exodus: 21, 93

F

finitude: 17, 86, 101, 103, 108, 109, 119
freedom: 9, 17, 18, 19, 28, 36, 38, 90, 97, 99, 102, 103, 105, 106, 107, 109, 110, 111, 112, 113, 118, 121
fundamentalism: 84

G

Gaudium et Spes: 4, 7, 55, 98, 121
God: 2, 3, 4, 8, 9, 10, 11, 13, 14, 15, 16, 17, 18, 19, 20, 21, 22, 23, 24, 25, 26, 27, 28, 29, 30, 31, 32, 33, 34, 35, 36, 37, 38, 41, 42, 43, 44, 45, 46, 47, 49, 50, 51, 52, 54, 55, 56, 57, 58, 59, 61, 62, 63, 64, 65, 72, 74, 75, 76, 77, 81, 85, 93, 94, 95, 98, 99, 100, 101, 102, 103, 104, 105, 106, 107, 108, 109, 110, 111, 112, 113, 114, 115, 116, 119, 120, 121, 122
Gospel: 31, 48, 61, 62, 67, 69, 71, 79, 114, 122
grace: 11, 15, 16, 19, 21, 22, 25, 26, 31, 32, 34, 55, 62, 63, 64, 65, 98, 99, 116, 121

H
habits: 59, 90
hermeneutics: 68, 79, 80, 91
hierarchy: 67, 69
historical-critical: 85, 87
history: 1, 8, 9, 14, 15, 16, 18, 21, 25, 29, 38, 39, 45, 46, 49, 55, 58, 62, 63, 64, 65, 66, 68, 73, 76, 77, 78, 79, 81, 82, 83, 85, 86, 88, 94, 98, 99, 103, 104, 105, 106, 111, 112, 113, 116, 117, 119
humanism: 48, 111
"humanum": 11, 80, 116
humility: 104
hypostasis: 112, 114
hypostatic: 65, 112, 113, 115

I
immutability: 98, 103, 106, 107
impassibility: 103
incarnation: 4, 9, 10, 11, 14, 24, 25, 26, 33, 34, 47, 51, 63, 75, 95, 96, 98, 100, 104, 108, 113, 115, 117, 122
independence: 15, 102, 103, 109, 112, 113, 115
infallible: 67
inspiration: 57, 122
intention: 16, 45, 46
intentionality: 11, 25, 26, 65, 66
interdependence: 39, 104, 117
intratextual: 85

J
Jesus: 4, 5, 9, 10, 11, 13, 19, 20, 21, 22, 23, 24, 25, 26, 27, 28, 29, 30, 31, 32, 33, 34, 35, 37, 41, 42, 43, 44, 45, 46, 47, 48, 49, 50, 52, 54, 55, 56, 57, 58, 59, 60, 61, 62, 63, 64, 66, 72, 80, 81, 86, 87, 93, 94, 95, 96, 97, 98, 103, 112, 113, 114, 115, 116, 117, 118, 119, 120, 121
John: 30, 90, 103, 114, 118
judgment: 45, 65, 122
justice: 1, 3, 11, 12, 13, 37, 54, 83, 88

K
kenosis: 101, 102, 107, 114, 115

L
law: 10, 11, 12, 18, 19, 22, 23, 24, 25, 26, 27, 28, 29, 30, 31, 32, 36, 48, 51, 53, 54, 55, 56, 57, 65, 89, 114
liberal: 58
liberation: 84, 88, 97, 111
life-praxis: 62
Logos: 63, 112, 113, 114, 122
Lutheran: 30, 53

M
magisterium: 68
Marxism: 3
mediation: 64, 67, 72, 82, 90
medieval: 27
metanoia: 79
mission: 20, 91, 121
morality: 1, 3, 8, 9, 10, 11, 12, 13, 17, 19, 23, 24, 25, 26, 27, 28, 29, 32, 37, 38, 39, 41, 42, 43, 48, 54, 55, 56, 57, 64, 65, 66, 67, 73, 75, 76, 78, 79, 85, 89, 94, 120, 121
motivation: 9, 11, 13, 22, 25, 40, 45, 61
Muslims: 42

N
non-Christian: 23, 82
norm: 2, 13, 18, 19, 22, 26, 30, 42, 54, 55, 89, 116
normative: 12, 13, 14, 24, 35, 45, 50, 64, 79, 81, 85
norms: 8, 9, 12, 22, 23, 28, 32, 49, 64, 65, 68, 91

O
obligations: 2, 43
ontological: 11, 27, 31, 33, 63, 112, 113, 119

P
paschal mystery: 93, 94, 119
Paul: 47, 48, 71, 93, 108, 111, 122

planetization: 1
plausibility: 85, 89
pluralism: 1, 7, 90
praxis: 20, 80, 88, 92, 93
proclamation; 59, 61
Protestant: 23, 29, 30, 34, 35, 37, 47, 48, 49, 52, 53, 54, 55, 56, 57, 58, 66, 67, 68

R

redemption: 11, 16, 24, 95, 96, 100, 117, 119
Reformation: 29
reformer: 20, 30
relativism: 50, 81, 87
religion: 3, 8, 34, 38, 45, 58, 63, 73, 83, 84, 97
resurrection: 22, 47
revelation: 4, 11, 14, 15, 21, 23, 24, 25, 26, 27, 30, 31, 33, 34, 35, 36, 41, 42, 44, 45, 46, 54, 55, 56, 57, 58, 59, 60, 66, 72, 73, 74, 80, 81, 85, 94, 97, 109, 116, 117, 118

S

sacraments: 75
salvation: 15, 16, 17, 18, 20, 21, 22, 29, 61, 62, 64, 76, 95, 96, 111, 116, 119, 122
Scripture: 3, 11, 12, 13, 17, 23, 25, 30, 33, 34, 46, 54, 56, 57, 58, 59, 66, 67, 71, 96
Scriptures: 12, 13, 25, 26, 30, 32, 45, 50, 56, 59, 69, 72
sectarianism: 83, 87
secularization: 7, 36
self-revelation: 122
socialization: 70, 71, 72, 73, 77, 97
solidarity: 21, 22
soteriology: 1, 95
spirituality: 19, 95
symbol: 74, 75, 84, 94, 119

T

theocentric: 23, 37, 45, 46, 47, 48, 52, 60
tradition: 2, 5, 7, 8, 23, 25, 26, 27, 31, 35, 37, 39, 40, 41, 45, 46, 50,

51, 53, 57, 58, 59, 62, 66, 68, 69, 70, 71, 72, 73, 75, 76, 77, 78, 79, 80, 81, 83, 84, 85, 86, 87, 88, 89, 90, 91, 92, 96, 97, 99, 112, 120

transcendence: 9, 14, 18, 62, 63, 99, 100, 101, 103, 115
trinitarian: 100
Trinity: 112
truth: 13, 20, 25, 31, 32, 35, 36, 40, 50, 51, 55, 58, 59, 62, 69, 73, 80, 84, 85, 86, 87, 88, 89, 90, 95, 100, 107, 112, 117, 120

U
universals: 46

V
virtue: 9, 15, 21, 33, 34, 49, 50, 65, 73, 112

Index

Authors

A
Aquinas, Thomas: 8, 27
Aristotle: 99, 103
Auer, A: 8, 9

B
Barr, James: 82
Barth, Karl: 30, 31, 32, 33, 34, 35, 36, 37, 44, 49, 54, 56, 58, 59, 60
Berdyaev, N.: 110
Bloch, Ernst: 111
Bonhoeffer, Dietrich: 4, 36
Brunner, Emil: 35, 36, 37
Bulgakov, S.: 102

C
Cahill, Lisa: 47, 70, 71
Calvin, John: 30
Cobb, John: 90
Cox, Harvey: 84
Curran, Charles: 8, 23, 24

D
Dawe, Donald: 106
Driver, Tom: 5

Dulles, Avery: 25, 74
Durkheim, E.: 75

E
Ellul, Jacques: 54

F
Fiorenza, Francis Schüssler: 61, 80, 91
Fischer, Kathleen: 74, 75
Fowler, James: 89
Fuchs, Josef: 10, 11, 12, 28, 37, 55

G
Gilkey, Langdon: 93
Groff, Warren: 117
Groom, Tom: 70
Gustafson, James: 29, 31, 37, 38, 39, 40, 41, 42, 43, 44, 45, 46, 47, 48, 56, 57, 59, 60, 72, 87

H
Habermas, Jurgen: 91
Haight, Roger: 16
Harnack, Adolph von: 61
Hauerwas, Stanley: 37, 49, 50, 51, 59
Hellwig, Monika: 117
Hodgson, Peter: 108, 110

J
Jaspers, Karl: 1
Jeremias, Joachim: 54

K
Kelsey, David: 33
Kraemer, Heinrich: 5
Küng, Hans: 10, 104

L

Lehmann, Paul: 111
Lindbeck, George: 83, 84, 85
Loisy, Alfred: 61, 63
Lovin, Rubin: 2
Luther, Martin: 29

M

MacGregor, George: 102
Macquarrie, John: 111, 118
Marechal, Joseph: 14
May, William: 26
McCormick, Richard: 24, 25, 28, 56, 57
Mead, Herbert: 70
Metz, Johann Baptist: 65, 114, 115
Moltmann, Jurgen: 104, 105
Musurillo, Herbert: 73

N

Niebuhr, H. Richard: 78

O

O'Donnell, John: 103
Ogletree, Thomas: 83

R

Rahner, Karl: 13, 14, 15, 16, 17, 18, 19, 25, 31, 32, 33, 36, 37, 42, 62, 63, 64, 65, 73, 84, 107, 112, 115
Ramsey, Paul: 47, 48

S

Sartre, Jean Paul: 110
Schillebeeckx, Edward: 10, 19, 20, 21, 22, 80, 81, 116, 120
Schleiermacher, Friedrich: 58
Schreiter, Robert: 69, 87, 88
Schuller, Bruno: 10, 12
Shoenfeld, W.: 54

Soelle, Dorothee: 5
Spohn, William: 78, 79

T
Tillich, Paul: 108
Tracy, David: 72
Troeltsch, Ernest: 72

W
Weil, Simone: 104